ROUTLEDGE LIBRARY EDITIONS:
FREE WILL AND DETERMINISM

Volume 10

THE REFUTATION OF DETERMINISM

THE REFUTATION OF DETERMINISM

An Essay in Philosophical Logic

M. R. AYERS

LONDON AND NEW YORK

First published in 1968 by Methuen & Co Ltd

This edition first published in 2017
by Routledge
2 Park Square, Milton Park, Abingdon, Oxon OX14 4RN

and by Routledge
711 Third Avenue, New York, NY 10017

Routledge is an imprint of the Taylor & Francis Group, an informa business

© 1968 M. R. Ayers

All rights reserved. No part of this book may be reprinted or reproduced or utilised in any form or by any electronic, mechanical, or other means, now known or hereafter invented, including photocopying and recording, or in any information storage or retrieval system, without permission in writing from the publishers.

Trademark notice: Product or corporate names may be trademarks or registered trademarks, and are used only for identification and explanation without intent to infringe.

British Library Cataloguing in Publication Data
A catalogue record for this book is available from the British Library

ISBN: 978-1-138-63228-8 (Set)
ISBN: 978-1-315-20086-6 (Set) (ebk)
ISBN: 978-1-138-73172-1 (Volume 10) (hbk)
ISBN: 978-1-138-73209-4 (Volume 10) (pbk)
ISBN: 978-1-315-18870-6 (Volume 10) (ebk)

Publisher's Note
The publisher has gone to great lengths to ensure the quality of this reprint but points out that some imperfections in the original copies may be apparent.

Disclaimer
The publisher has made every effort to trace copyright holders and would welcome correspondence from those they have been unable to trace.

M. R. AYERS

THE REFUTATION OF DETERMINISM

An Essay in Philosophical Logic

METHUEN & CO LTD

First published 1968 by Methuen & Co Ltd
11 New Fetter Lane, EC4
© 1968 M. R. Ayers
Printed in Great Britain by
Butler & Tanner Ltd, Frome and London

Distributed in the U.S.A. by Barnes & Noble Inc.

Contents

	PREFACE	*page* vii
1	INTRODUCTION	1
2	PROBABILITY AND POSSIBILITY FOR CHOICE	12
	1 Introductory	12
	2 A theory about personal power	14
	3 A criticism of Keynes	18
	4 Some more theories about personal power	25
	5 An analogy between two kinds of possibility	33
3	PROBABILITY AND NATURAL POWERS	38
	1 Introductory	38
	2 The relation between epistemic and natural possibility	38
	3 A criticism of the doctrine that 'probable' is ambiguous	42
	4 A comparison of possibility with probability	50
4	SOME UNOBSERVABLE PROPERTIES	55
	1 Introductory	55
	2 Certainty, necessity and Hume	55
	3 Epistemology and determinism	60
	4 An analysis proposed and defended	68
	5 Power and law	75
5	SOME PUZZLES ABOUT POTENTIALITY	80
	1 Introductory	80
	2 The idea of a 'circumstance'	80
	3 The distinction between intrinsic and extrinsic properties	84
	4 The refutation of actualism	89
	5 The refutation of the theory that 'all power is conditional'	95

6 THE POWERS OF PEOPLE AND THE POWERS OF THINGS — 102
1. Introductory — 102
2. The distinction between natural and personal power — 103
3. The refutation of Ryle's dispositionalist account of human capacities — 106

7 IFS AND CANS — 119
1. Introductory — 119
2. The refutation of the theory that all personal power is conditional — 119
3. A refutation of the orthodox account of 'I can', as equivalent to a conditional statement — 125
4. A contradiction in dispositionalism — 135
5. Further objections to the orthodox view — 138
6. The verification of 'I can': more about trying — 144

8 DELIBERATION, FREEDOM AND MEANING — 151
1. Introductory — 151
2. More about possibility and the context of deliberation; and about the relation between power and will — 151
3. On not being able to help it: a discussion of the relationship between power and responsibility — 162
4. On the meaning of words like 'can' — 169

BIBLIOGRAPHY — 181

INDEX — 183

Preface

Perhaps everyone who can think has the concept of possibility, but no one understands it. Determinism, the metaphysical theory that everything is necessarily as it is and that there are no genuinely open possibilities beyond what actually happens, is a symptom of this lack of understanding. The weakness of the arguments of those who oppose Determinism is an indication that the lack is universal. It is the contention of this book that possibility is a concept which can be understood, and that when it is understood Determinism will shed its plausibility. For in spite of all its paradox, Determinism possesses a plausibility that cannot readily be undermined.

There is only one method for attaining this understanding, and that is by argument. We can appeal to no criterion or standard in the course of this argument, except to a sense of what is reasonable. Philosophy is only for those who are prepared to use their judgement outside any rules. As a serious study, it is also only for those who are ready to treat emotionally arid and practically useless subjects with care and without contempt, for the sake of clarity and truth. The freewill dilemma is traditionally a problem for 'moral philosophy', but like most problems for this artificial specialism its solution demands hard work in less popularly appealing fields.

Throughout the variety of topics discussed, I have tried to maintain a consecutive thread of argument. I do not suppose that the argument is perfectly complete: I am not sure what it would be like to have said the last word on a philosophical question. I do think that the argument is new, even if not at every point entirely new. I do not think that my solution of the freewill problem, or my main criticisms of previously attempted solutions, have been offered by anyone else.

While I cannot say that any important part of the work was directly suggested by any writer, I am aware that I have been helped to develop my ideas by a number of books, including the writings of G. E. M. Anscombe, John Austin, Stuart Hampshire, R. M. Hare, and Richard Taylor. Other debts are acknowledged in the text. The theme of Hampshire's recent book *The Freedom of the Individual* perhaps comes closest to my own, but its appearance in 1965 has not affected the present work. In any case, although that book succeeds in raising in a short space many of the right questions about possibility, its argument appears to me to suffer from some serious deficiencies.

I have often referred to the arguments of particular philosophers, living and dead, but never with the intention of giving a full history of any doctrine or a complete picture of present opinion. I have made wide use of quotation and the method of criticism only because it has seemed helpful in the presentation of my own theories, and in demonstrating the significance of the issues under discussion.

An early draft of the work was presented in 1962 as a dissertation for a Research Fellowship at St John's College, Cambridge, and a fuller version in 1963 as a Ph.D. thesis. I am grateful to the Master and Fellows of St John's for my election to the Research Fellowship, which enabled me to devote more time to the subject of the work than would otherwise have been possible. I must also express my debt to the Department of Philosophy of the University of California, Berkeley, and to the Moral Science Faculty of the University of Cambridge, for making it possible for me to undergo the discipline of expounding my arguments to quick-witted and critical student audiences, without which I should have written a far more obscure and incomplete book.

I have profited from the criticisms and suggestions of those who have read drafts of parts or of the whole of the book. They include Renford Bambrough, I. M. Crombie, A. C. Ewing, A. I. Melden, Gilbert Ryle and John Wisdom. I am particularly indebted to Professor Wisdom for help in the early stages, and to Professor Ryle both for his general criticisms which led to the final shape of the work and for his careful and detailed comments on the penultimate draft.

My deepest acknowledgement is to John Wisdom and Renford Bambrough, to whom I owe both my interest in philosophy and my respect for its difficulties.

Wadham College, 1967   M. R. A.

I

Introduction

In spite of its title, the primary aim of this book is constructive. It is to offer a reasonable and explanatory account of the concept of potentiality and related concepts. The freewill problem is certainly the heaviest millstone around the neck of anyone who inquires into the nature of potentiality, and it is impossible to imagine a satisfactory treatment of either the concept or the problem that does not involve the other at a fundamental level. But a well-known remark about *can*, that in philosophy we seem so often to uncover it, 'just when we had thought some problem settled, grinning residually up at us like the frog at the bottom of the beer mug', is right in its suggestion that a careful investigation of possibility and potentiality is likely to be philosophically rewarding in many areas of dispute.

It is my constructive purpose that will largely determine the order of exposition in what follows. Consequently my critical purpose, which is primarily the refutation of the arguments that give rise to the freewill dilemma, may seem to be pursued in a rather haphazard and subordinate way. My preferred method of warfare may often seem to be sniping rather than frontal assault. As an aid to orientation, I shall start by directly considering some of the crude but compelling reasoning on the basis of which determinism is usually advanced. I shall take a glance at the wood from this too familiar viewpoint, before properly coming to grips with the trees.

The common premiss of both determinist and indeterminist is, of course, the alleged incompatibility of causation and freedom of choice. This supposition is usually supported by the argument that, if an event is in all respects causally explicable, then it could not have been any different, since to explain an event completely just *is* to shew that nothing else was possible in the circumstances. If one thing is the whole cause of another, then given the occurrence of the first thing, the other *must* occur. This is the meaning of 'cause'. Likewise, to say that something is a law is to say that anything different is impossible. So if everything that happens is governed by a law, nothing that fails to happen is possible, or ever was possible. On the other hand, everyone agrees, or should agree, that for there to be freedom of choice or, therefore, any real choice at all, the agent must be presented with alternatives that are all genuine possibilities. It follows that a free choice cannot be causally determined, and it can have no complete explanation.

Some may think that this argument is simply absurd, but it can appear almost as plausible as it is well-known. I shall contend that is fallacious, but I shall also contend that all attempts to explain what is wrong with it have been inadequate. Any argument of which this is true deserves respect. Although it may not be explicitly involved in every formulation of determinism, I shall call it the 'Basic Argument' for determinism.

The 'Basic Argument', as so far expounded, presents us, of course, with a dilemma. Either we accept that actions are causally explicable, in which case we are committed to the startling proposition that there is no such thing as free choice, and nobody is ever really responsible for his actions; or else we protest that, since we obviously do often or at least sometimes act freely and know it, we can only conclude that some of our actions are in some respects uncaused. At this stage in the argument, the indeterminist's position might well seem the stronger. He does not, like the determinist, deny something that seems to be certainly true. He merely makes a definite assertion about a subject on which we might suppose a lack of anything like complete evidence. His assertion is surprising and may seem in some way repugnant to reason. Nevertheless, apart from further developments in the dispute, the least that could be said for the indeterminist would be that he is less unreasonable than the determinist.

It should perhaps be mentioned that we do not avoid difficulties by withholding judgement between determinist and indeterminist, for this impartiality itself involves adopting the view that we do not know whether we are ever responsible for our actions. It is nearly, if not equally as paradoxical to assert that nobody ever knows that he can do an action unless he actually performs it, as it is to say that no action ever is possible unless it is actually performed. In other words, the Basic Argument can figure as part of an argument for a kind of metaphysical scepticism, which is about as puzzling and paradoxical a philosophical doctrine as any other. Our dilemma is really a trilemma.

There are, however, a number of additional arguments designed to make determinism the most attractive theory. Some of these arguments are now rightly regarded as feeble or fallacious. For example it has been supposed that it can be known *a priori* that 'every event has a cause', either because this proposition is logically necessary or because it is some kind of necessary presupposition of scientific, or any other kind of thought. Such a view is based on arguments that may be of great interest but that no longer have a wide appeal. I shall not discuss them. Another typical attempt to bully us into agreeing that every action is completely caused is based on a philosophy of mind that nowadays, if it is not always seen as palpably naïve, is at least generally viewed with strong suspicion. In its exteme form, every action is represented as necessarily entirely the result of an entity called a 'strongest motive' or 'greatest desire', a mental spring that provides the energy for the curious, irreversible clockwork of choice, volition and act. This mechanistic theory of mind is not convincing.

Nevertheless, even if some of his guns misfire, the determinist can call on an argument that really does seem extremely powerful, and that might seem to make his doctrine invulnerable. It is a sort of *reductio ad absurdum* of indeterminism, which runs more or less as follows. Let us suppose that some human actions are not caused, that they are indetermined and so really could have been otherwise. This is simply to suppose them accidental, random, unpredictable and unrelated to the agent's personality. How can we even ascribe such an event to an agent as an action of his, unless it can be related to his character and past performances? How can we judge it, unless we can relate it to a specific and intelligible motive, and how can we do this if it is a bolt from the blue? It was a complaint against the determinist Hobbes that the only kind of 'liberty' he allowed within his system was the kind of freedom a river has to flow down its channel; but the indeterminist must face the complaint that he gives us nothing more than the freedom of a microparticle to move at random. Why should a man be held responsible for something supposed to be unrelated to all antecedents and perhaps to all that comes afterwards, something that came into his head from nowhere?

On the other hand, responsibility certainly does require that the agent could have done otherwise. The only conclusion left to draw, it is argued, is one drawn by C. D. Broad in a classic formulation of this argument,[1] that responsibility and freedom of choice are self-contradictory notions, requiring that an agent both could and could not have acted otherwise, that his action both was and was not causally determined. Determinism, if this is the right name for the doctrine that no person is ever responsible for his actions or ever makes a free choice, is no longer presented as the lesser of two evils, the more acceptable horn of a dilemma, but as the only possible conclusion of a rigorous argument. It is also, interestingly enough, made wholly independent of what is also sometimes not unreasonably called 'determinism': the view simply that every event has a scientific explanation. It should be understood that it is the first kind of determinism that I am concerned to refute. Where it is necessary, I shall mark the distinction by calling the denial of the existence of any free choice 'metaphysical determinism', and the view that everything that happens is in principle explicable by reference to its antecedents and laws of nature, 'scientific determinism'.

The charge that indeterminism would merely make some actions random and inexplicable events, not really personally significant actions at all, has been and remains, I think, the strongest obstacle to its acceptance, largely explaining the relative popularity of determinism among English-speaking philosophers. No satisfactory answer has been given. Even if, in their presentation of the argument, determinists have sometimes misrepresented 'motives' as ghostly thrusts logically required to trigger off actions, or 'character' as a pre-existing and wholly determinate substrate uniquely determining them, or laws of nature as ubiquitous tram-lines through time, nothing at all seems to be achieved by the indeterminist's mysterious notion of 'contra-causal' choice towards a more reasonable and accurate philosophical account of choice, action and the logic of the explanation of action. If the determinist often talks as if a human being is the helpless onlooker and victim of the clanking machinery of his own mind and body, set apart

[1] 'Determinism, Indeterminism & Libertarianism' in C. D. Broad: *Ethics and the History of Philosophy*.

in some unintelligible way from his own plannings and decidings, the indeterminist has even more notoriously seen the situation in the same terms, with the single difference that the Self is now supposed capable of twitching a metaphysical muscle occasionally in order to deflect those plannings. The picture of the transcendent agent is not convincing, and it is a more plausible theory that to call an action mine is at least to bring it into relation with my past actions and the personality that I and others know. Nothing very clear or persuasive has been brought against this point in the determinist's position.

It is the thesis of this book, however, that an earlier part of the argument is fallacious, the 'Basic Argument' that presents the dilemma. This is not a particularly original view in itself, for the forces of compromise have a long history in the dispute, and have recently been largely victorious. We shall see that these peacemakers tend to commit the same mistakes as the extremists. But it must be admitted that they do very often direct critical attention to the right place – the steps taken in the Basic Argument. I shall discuss the most popular remedies in detail later on, but it may help to consider some suggestions now. It may help us to see what determinism is.

Hobbes offers a definition of 'liberty', which we need not go into, but according to which a man may be said to do an action freely even though he acted necessarily and could not have acted otherwise, at least in any categorical sense. In other words, Hobbes attacks that premiss of the Basic Argument that seems to be its strongest, the premiss that, for there to be freedom of action, the agent must be presented with alternatives that are genuine possibilities. Hobbes is nevertheless renowned as a determinist, and, I think, rightly so. One reason is simply that he is a scientific determinist, and indeed argues that it is necessarily true that every event has a cause. But he is also regarded as a determinist because his view that no one ever could have done anything, except what he did, really leaves no room for 'liberty'. Hobbes thought otherwise, but in any case the assertion that every action that is performed is necessary or unavoidable is at least as paradoxical as the assertion that there is no liberty. So although Hobbes may reject a part of the 'Basic Argument' as it is formulated above, it is justifiable to call him and anyone else who goes so far as to hold that everyone acts necessarily, and could not act differently, a 'determinist'. More precisely, I shall call this kind of view *necessitarianism* (i.e. the view that everything happens necessarily, and everyone has to do what he does) or *actualism* (i.e. the view that nobody ever could do anything different, except what he actually does, and, in general, that only the actual is possible). It is 'actualism' that I shall mostly be concerned with, when I talk of 'determinism'. It should also be said that I shall very often neglect the fact that a philosopher who accepts the Basic Argument could as well be an indeterminist as a determinist, and I shall treat a refutation of the Basic Argument as a 'refutation of determinism'. The doctrine that if everything is caused, everything happens necessarily and so no one ever could act otherwise, might equally well be a part of an argument for indeterminism as for determinism, but I shall refer to it as a determinist doctrine, partly for the sake of brevity. A further justification for this practice is that indeterminism is a negative theory, as its name indicates, and parasitic on determinism. Philosophers are frightened into indeterminism by the bogey of determinism, and we are justified in regarding the determinist as our main adversary.

It may seem very surprising, but it is possible to be a determinist in virtue of being an actualist, without also being a necessitarian. Hume, or at any rate the position that Hume seems most inclined to adopt, is a case in point. Many people have thought that his account of causation undermines the Basic Argument radically, since he denies that an effect ever really follows its cause necessarily. It is still an argument of some who offer resolutions of the 'free-will' dilemma, that, in introducing the notion of necessary connections between events, the determinist has simply confused the causal relation ('constant conjunction') with logical implication, and has allowed a logical *must* to creep into a non-logical argument. It is true that many determinists are open to this charge, and they are always vulnerable to Humean criticism. But their mistake is not an essential element of the Basic Argument. For one thing, there is a concept of non-logical, 'natural' or 'empirical' necessity, which is not, as Hume thought, purely subjective. To say that an event is necessary is simply to say that it is not possible that it should not take place. If the Humean insists that such a notion makes no sense, the question to ask is whether he admits empirical, as well as logical, possibility. If he does allow that there is such a thing, as most now would, then the Basic Argument can easily be formulated for his benefit entirely in terms of possibility, without bringing in the correlative term 'necessary'. If, however, the Humean follows his master in questioning even the notion of empirical possibility, then he has already arrived, by a short cut, at the determinist (actualist) position that there are no real possibilities beyond what actually happens, unless what is meant is logical possibilities. Hume's actualism will receive much fuller discussion later, but the fact is that exactly the same epistemology as leads him to deny necessity in events, also leads him, as in all consistency it should, to limit his conception of possibility and potentiality so severely that it is one of his central doctrines that 'the distinction between a power and its exercise is entirely frivolous'. That is to say, the Humean attack on the notion of necessity, popular as it is in discussions of freewill, not only fails to provide a satisfactory answer to determinism, but even breeds a separate argument for it. This argument will later be of particular interest in the attempt to give an analysis of potentiality.

G. E. Moore was another peacemaker. In a famous passage (*Ethics*, Ch. 7) Moore makes two important moves, neither of which is entirely original to him. The first is extremely simple, but none the less important. He emphasises the *prima facie* unacceptability of the consequences of the determinist's claim that if every action is caused then no one ever could have acted otherwise. He brings it forcibly before our minds that this claim is in conflict with what no sane man would normally doubt, that there really is a distinction holding between what people (and for that matter, cats or ships) can do, and what they cannot do, even among the things that they do not do. It does seem more probable, to say the least, that something is wrong with the bewildering metaphysical argument presented to us by the determinist, than that the propositions that I could have walked a mile in twenty minutes this morning, and that a particular ship could have steamed twenty knots on a particular occasion, are bound to be false unless these performances actually took place. Moore's appeals to 'common-sense', of which this is one, are the topic of much debate, often being condemned as mere denials of what is asserted, or praised as an appeal to a subtle (but, as it seems, incorrect) theory of meaning. In fact their force stems very largely from the reminder that it can be certain that an argument is invalid, even if we cannot say exactly what is wrong with it – a simple point that is frequently forgotten in the heat of debate.

Moore goes on to improve his case by a second move, which is simply a suggestion as to the kind of fallacy the determinist has committed. He suggests that the words 'can' and 'could' are ambiguous, and that the Basic Argument hinges on this ambiguity.

It is easy to see how this might be so, simply by considering the move from, say,

A. *If every event is caused, no event ever could have been otherwise than it was* to

B. *If every event is caused, nothing could ever do anything that it does not actually do.*

If language is ever anything to go by, there is obviously some ground for distinguishing the meaning of 'could' as it appears in A from its meaning in B. For example, in B it might be replaced by 'has the power to' without any apparent change in meaning. But the same transposition in A would not even produce sense, since events neither have nor lack powers, except perhaps such odd powers as the power to surprise people. It is interesting that Hobbes does argue directly for the proposition that nothing ever possesses a power unless it actually 'produces' the appropriate act (*Elements of Philosophy*, Ch. X, especially sections 3 and 4). His argument is worth special consideration, but it is undeniably less plausible than one that uses only 'possible' or 'can'. It is not really very convincing to be told, in effect, that if there is (as no doubt there is) an explanation for a car's doing 60 m.p.h. on some occasion, then it follows that the car lacked the power to do 80 m.p.h. or even, remarkably enough, a steady 50 m.p.h. It seems somehow more attractive to suppose that the event 'could not have been otherwise' than that the car lacked the power to perform differently. This alone should make us wonder whether 'could' is not more slippery than seems to be envisaged by one who propounds the Basic Argument.

We should surely be even more suspicious of the move from either A or B to

C. *If every event is caused, no person ever could do anything that he does not actually do.*

For we certainly talk in a way to suggest that the ability of a person to do something is a different kind of thing from the 'powers' of inanimate objects. We even talk in ways that suggest, and have suggested to the author of the entry under *can* in the *Oxford English Dictionary*, that we do not always mean the same thing by 'can' with a personal subject. For example, 'He could do it' may sometimes be replaced, without altering the sense, by 'He is capable of doing it', sometimes by 'He is in a position to do it', and sometimes by 'He has the opportunity to do it', but these do not all mean the same. *Opportunity* is a notable example of a concept closely related to *possibility*, but that can have nothing but a wildly metaphorical application outside a personal sphere. Another is *choice*. Again, while there is nothing strange about 'He can either do it or not', there is an odd ring to 'This car can either do 50 m.p.h. or not', where this is not merely the tautology, 'Either it can do 50 or it can not'. We cannot simply say that it is false, for it is as odd to deny as to assert it.

These somewhat random linguistic considerations are not offered as conclusive arguments, nor even as arguments at all, but simply in order to raise a doubt. Should we not at least wonder whether there is not more than one concept of possibility involved in the determinist's train of thought, some unrecognised but vital distinction?

One of the determinist's most powerful subsidiary arguments can be turned against him here. He rightly complains that nothing is achieved towards explaining responsibility and choice by the hypothesis of indeterminism, randomness or unpredictability. But this persuasive point can equally well be applied to possibility and power. An action which lacked a cause would not *thereby* be under the agent's control. In that case, we need to think hard what sense can be attributed to the claim that he would thereby be able not to perform it, that it would be within his power not to do it, or indeed, that he could do otherwise. None of these things would *follow* from the supposition that an action was not predictable, or not causally explicable. Yet in the 'Basic Argument' the determinist seems to be using, or seems to need, a notion of possibility such that for one thing to be the sufficient cause of another simply means that if the one occurs the other 'cannot but' occur. In such a use, of course, if an event is uncaused, it *follows* that it could have been otherwise. But if, as it is assumed, 'If an event was caused, it could not have been otherwise' is merely less specific than 'If an action was caused, the agent could not have refrained from doing it', then from the converse, namely, 'If an event was uncaused, it could have been otherwise', we could deduce the unacceptable conclusion 'If an action was uncaused, the agent could have done otherwise.' It is unacceptable for just the same sorts of reason as a determinist such as Broad will advance against the view that indeterminism is sufficient to account for responsibility and freedom. What the determinist fails to recognise is that this inadequacy is a sign that some sort of equivocation, or something analogous to equivocation, may be involved in his own step from the 'impossibility' of events, to the powerlessness of people.

As Moore recognised, what is required in order to clinch the case against determinism at this point is a systematic demonstration that there are such significantly different concepts of possibility, or, if it is preferred, such significant differences within the concept of possibility. This I shall endeavour to provide. Moore's own chief suggestion in this direction, however, which derives from Hobbes and Hume, to go back no further, and which is probably still the most popular of all would-be resolutions of the freewill problem, is that the 'I could . . .' that is relevant to freewill has a special sense, being equivalent to 'I could . . ., if I chose' or 'I should . . ., if I chose.' This kind of explanation, although not without plausibility, is fundamentally mistaken, and I shall argue that it suffers from much the same confusion as determinism and indeterminism.

Be that as it may, the Basic Argument contains another error, which Moore evidently did not appreciate. For a general misconception of the nature of potentiality and possibility manifests itself even in the proposition that according to Moore 'obviously follows' from the premiss that every event has a cause: namely, the proposition that 'in *one* sense of the word "could", nothing ever *could* have happened, except what did happen'. Any attempt to explain the errors of actualism here would simply anticipate a necessarily long argument. It is the kind of mistake involved in Hume's contention that the distinction between a power and its exercise is entirely frivolous, or in Hobbes' principle that all power is conditional.

My intention is, then, roughly speaking, to try to bring home to the determinist, and others, two sorts of mistake. I shall try to show that the determinist characteristically confuses different kinds of possibility, and that he misunderstands even the kinds that he recognises. It will be found that it is an oversimplification to treat the first mistake as a fallacy of equivocation, as Moore suggests.

It must be confessed that the dialectic of determinism is capable of an indefinite number of more or less subtle variations. This is especially so in the region of philosophical psychology. It need hardly be said that I shall not investigate them all. The issues I shall discuss are, it is hoped, sufficiently central for my purpose. Finally, it should be emphasised that the refutation of determinism is only one of the aims of this book, even in its critical and subordinate aspect.

2

Probability and Possibility for Choice

1. INTRODUCTORY

That there are different kinds of possibility is something hardly in dispute among philosophers. Few would now fail to recognise at least the distinction between logical and non-logical possibility, or to ascribe to it the greatest importance if any clarity at all is to be achieved in discussions of possibility. I shall not be very much concerned with this particular distinction, however, partly just because it is so widely recognised. The three chief kinds of possibility that I shall examine in most detail are all non-logical. I shall start with a brief description of them, which will fulfil the secondary function of explaining some terminology.

The first kind of possibility to be discussed is sometimes called 'epistemic possibility', but I shall also call it 'relative possibility', for reasons that should become clear. The sentences 'It is possible that it will rain tomorrow' and 'He might possibly call tomorrow', as normally used, would express relative possibility-statements.

The second kind of possibility is 'natural possibility'. I shall avoid the commonly used expression 'empirical possibility', which strongly insinuates the mistake that many writers make, when they suppose that possibility-statements of this type are the *only* empirical or non-logical possibility-statements, a view with which I shall heartily disagree. The use of the term 'natural' which follows another fairly common practice among philosophers, is not intended to suggest a contrast with anything supernatural, or unnatural, or even conventional, but is adopted just because it is less misleading than 'empirical' and does usefully mark the connection between natural possibility and 'laws of nature'. An expression that is sometimes used, 'nomic possibility', suggests too close a connection with laws, and insinuates the mistaken view that all natural possibility-statements are general or universal. An example of a natural possibility-statement would be 'It is not possible that life should exist on the sun.' I shall also talk of the related concepts of 'natural necessity', 'natural power' and 'natural potentiality'. An example of an attribution of a natural power would be a proposition expressed by 'This car can do 100 m.p.h.', taken in its normal sense.

Thirdly, I shall distinguish a general kind of possibility that I shall call 'possibility for choice'. An example of this kind of possibility-statement would be 'It is possible for him to come to dinner tonight', which might also be expressed 'He could come . . .' or 'It is in his power to come . . .' Consequently it may be described as an ascription of a power to a person, or, simply, an ascription of 'personal power'.

It is, of course, my contention that no possibility-statement can belong to more than one of these categories, but this classification is certainly not intended to be exhaustive, and is only generic. Both outside it and within it there is variety, which will sometimes be adumbrated.

The most controversial aspect of this terminology is likely to be the sharp and significant distinction that it implies between natural possibility and possibility for choice, between natural powers and personal powers. This is certainly the most important distinction and on it depends the most important part of what I shall say about the freewill problem, but it will not be explained until the later chapters. A question perhaps arises about the reasons for the discussion of epistemic possibility. It may seem that anyone can avoid confusing the proposition that it is possible that Smith will call with the proposition that it is possible for Smith to call. Why then is there a long disquisition on the distinction?

Firstly, surprising though it may be, such a confusion plays a significant role in the thinking of a number of excellent philosophers on the subject of possibility. Discussions of power and potentiality, especially as they occur in the freewill controversy, are fairly haunted by the notion of epistemic possibility, and the related notions of certainty and uncertainty, predictability and unpredictability. This is not mere confusion, for cogent-seeming arguments can be advanced for the view that the explanation of the notion of personal power is to be found in an inability to predict action. It is therefore necessary to be fairly clear on the nature of epistemic possibility, and on its relation to the other kinds of possibility. This clarification will provide a starting-point for an account of natural possibility and possibility for choice.

Secondly, it may be an advantage to start by considering mistaken theories about possibility in an area not, perhaps, at the very centre of the controversy. It will be encouraging if it can be demonstrated that a measure of clarity is enough to refute at least some intuitively objectionable metaphysical doctrines.

2. A THEORY ABOUT PERSONAL POWER

Moore remarks that there is a sense of 'possible' in which,

> whenever we have several different courses of action in view, it is *possible* for us to choose any one of them ... This sense arises from the fact that in such cases we can hardly ever *know for certain* beforehand, *which* choice we actually *shall* make; and one of the commonest senses of the word 'possible' is that in which we call an event 'possible' when no man can *know for certain* that it will not happen. (op. cit., p. 136.)

Moore is cautious enough not to commit himself to the view that this sense of 'possible' is relevant to the justification of an assertion that, as he puts it, 'we have Free Will', but he is also too cautious to reject it. In fact he is evidently offering his suggestion as a possible solution to the freewill problem, a way of avoiding the paradoxes of determinism and indeterminism: since if we say that it is possible that it will rain tomorrow, we certainly do not imply that the weather, however it turns out, will not be caused.

Moore's suggestion is, however, a very strange one. Even the attempt to make it has involved him in a significant linguistic solecism. No one who meant to imply that no man can know for certain that Smith will not call, would use the sentence 'It is possible *for* Smith to call' instead of the sentence 'It is possible *that* Smith will call.' These sentences obviously normally mean two different things, and it seems equally evident that neither proposition entails the other. But this short way with Moore's theory may seem to beg too many questions, and so we shall go more slowly.

Hume is one of those philosophers who accept as true what Moore offers as a suggestion. Hume is an actualist, and one objection to actualism is that it leaves unexplained why we should ever want to distinguish between the ability to act and the action itself, or ever want to say that someone has a power at all. Why should we imagine ourselves to be talking correctly and significantly, and very often justifiably and truly, when we say that someone could do something but will not, or could have done it but did not? We are often prepared to attribute to a person both the power of performing and the power of refraining from a particular action at a particular time. Yet it is logically certain that one of these powers will not be exercised, and either the doing or the not doing of the action will necessarily remain a potentiality.

Determinists, of course, will refuse to regard this as a serious objection – otherwise they would hardly be determinists – but they nevertheless often try to say something to weaken it. Hume is no exception. He accepts the fact of vulgar unphilosophical linguistic usage, but offers an explanation of the common 'error', which, he admits, 'proceeds not entirely from the scholastic doctrine of freewill'. If my enemy comes across me unarmed, he says, I do not suppose him free to harm me, as the law provides a strong motive to restrain him, and I know that he will not do so. If, however, there is no such motive, and therefore a possibility of his injuring me, I ascribe to him power over me. If I am *uncertain* whether he will or not, I 'suppose a possibility either of his acting or forbearing'. He continues, '... tho' in general we may conclude him to be determin'd by motives and causes, yet this removes not the uncertainty of our judgement concerning these causes, nor the influence of that uncertainty on the passions'.

Whether Hume supposes that uncertainty about the future may provide a justification as well as a causal explanation of our sometimes attributing to a man the power of choosing between possibilities, is perhaps not entirely clear. He has a well-known tendency to misrepresent himself as simply giving the psychological explanation of the judgements and inferences we make, rather than as offering an account of what would justify them. This is certainly so in the case of his theory of probability. At any rate he continues:

> Since therefore we ascribe a power of performing an action to every one who has no very powerful motive to forbear it, and refuse it to such as have; it may justly be concluded that *power* has always a reference to its *exercise*, either actual or probable, and that we consider a person as endow'd with any ability when we find from past experience that 'tis probable, or at least possible he may exert it ... power consists in the possibility or probability of any action, as discover'd by experience and practice of the world. (*Treatise*, p. 313.)[1]

This passage implies that he is willing to accept an important modification of the conceptual claim that power consists purely in its *actual* exercise, from which it cannot justifiably be distinguished. Yet in the paragraph following he seems to return to his previous strict equation of the two, again with the suggestion that, in pointing to its source in subjective uneasiness, he is giving nothing but a psychological explanation of vulgar and mistaken usage. Uncertainty is represented as a state of mind, the presence of which would merely provide a causal explanation of my *erroneous* supposition that the man who does not in the event harm me nevertheless had the power of doing me an injury: '... And tho' perhaps I never really feel any harm, and discover by the event, that, philosophically speaking, the person never had any power of harming me; since he did not exert any; this prevents not my uneasiness from the preceding uncertainty.' Yet if it were true that the power to act consisted, as a matter of logic, in 'the possibility or probability of any action', then I would not be proven to have been in error in supposing a man to have a certain power, merely by the fact that it was not actually exercised. For it may be the case that it was possible that he would act, even if he did not in fact do so. That is why it seems that Hume has in this paragraph slipped back into his previous account of power as indistinguishable from its *actual* exercise. But in reality he is not guilty of inconsistency or vacillation, since he holds a theory about probability itself according to which, if something does not happen, it cannot be said that it was *really* probable. Probability

---

[1] Page refs are to L. A. Selby-Bigge's edition, Oxford, 1888.

itself, according to Hume's usual view in the *Treatise*, is not a 'philosophical' or real relation, and probability statements are simply the expression of subjective states of expectation, which, strictly speaking, are incapable of justification. Because of this misconception about probability, Hume loses what might seem a great advantage of his modified theory of power, which is that a sense would be granted to the statement that a man could have acted otherwise than he did, so that it would no longer need to be regarded as self-contradictory.

According to Hume's theory of probability, the statement that a horse has won a race would entail the statement that there was no possibility ('philosophically speaking') that it would lose. This kind of absurdity is avoided by the standard theory that 'probability is relative to evidence', which is summed up in the following passage by Lord Keynes, one of its best-known proponents:

> There is nothing novel in the supposition that the probability of a theory turns upon the evidence by which it is supported; and it is common to assert that an opinion was probable on the evidence at first to hand, but on further information was untenable. As our knowledge or our hypothesis changes, our conclusions have new probabilities, not in themselves, but relatively to these new premisses. New logical relations have now become important, namely those between the conclusions which we are investigating and our new assumptions; but the old relations between the conclusions and the former assumptions still exist and are just as real as these new ones. It would be as absurd to deny that an opinion *was* probable, when at a later stage certain objections have come to light, as to deny, when we have reached our destination, that it was ever three miles distant; and the opinion still *is* probable in relation to the old hypotheses, just as the destination is still three miles from our starting-point. (*A Treatise on Probability*, p. 7.)

It is easy to see that Hume's theory that power consists in the probability or possibility of its exercise might be retained, while his paradoxical conclusion that, if a man does not harm me, then it follows that he never had the power of doing so, might yet be avoided. For if relatively to some set of evidence it is uncertain whether so-and-so will harm me, whatever happens later it will still be true that, relatively to that body of evidence, it was uncertain what he would do. Thus the equation of power with the possibility or probability of its exercise provides an account of the former that might seem compatible with rigid causal determination.

3. A CRITICISM OF KEYNES

If anyone wants to show that the sentence 'Although he did not go, he could have gone' normally means 'Although he did not go, it was possible that he would go', he must, of course, do more than appeal to the fact that both make sense and both often express truths. Some very obvious difficulties arise if we identify them and also accept a Keynesian explanation of epistemic possibility.

On the one hand, it would appear to follow that whatever a man does, and in whatever circumstances he does it – even if he is physically coerced and, as we should normally say, quite powerless to do otherwise – it will nevertheless always be possible for him to have done otherwise. For in every case it will be uncertain, relatively to some limited set or other of true evidential propositions, what he is going to do. On the other hand, there may be, and according to scientific determinism there always is, some other set, known or unknown, in relation to which any action is quite certain. Consequently it would seem to follow that, unless we have some clear principle to guide us in choosing the appropriate body of evidence, whether we say in any case that a man could or could not have acted otherwise depends entirely on some arbitrary decision on our part. To put it mildly, the theory presents a problem: in relation to what body of evidence are we supposed to judge whether a man could have acted otherwise, in those cases in which such a judgement is of practical or moral importance?

Now if we take this question seriously we risk the impatient reaction that we are wasting time, since obviously no epistemic possibility-statement is equivalent to any statement to the effect that a man had the power to do otherwise than he did. The latter just obviously is not 'relative to evidence', whatever exactly this may mean. But if our purpose is not simply to make this distinction intuitively, but also to understand the relation between the two sorts of possibility – why, for example, the word 'possible' can be used to make two such different statements – it will suit it to press the question. If the question is absurd, we want to know more fully why it is absurd.

There are answers to the question that are not entirely implausible. For one thing, it is not totally unlike another question that often gets short answers: what principle defines the body of evidence to which is relative such a perfectly straightforward probability-statement as the statement that it will probably rain tomorrow? It is clear that the answer to the question whether rain is likely, or, in Hume's example, whether it was possible that my enemy would harm me, would not depend on an arbitrary selection of evidential propositions, any more than the answer to the question whether my enemy could harm me.

The explanation usually given of the statement 'Rain is likely' is that it is relative to the evidence possessed by the speaker at the time. As one authority has it, 'the reason why we may easily overlook the relation of probability to evidence is that in ordinary life we commonly state probabilities in relation to all the knowledge we have at the time and therefore feel no need to specify the evidence. In other words our probability statements are commonly elliptical.'[1] We can take this to allow that the question whether something *was* probable is answerable relatively to some specifiable body of knowledge possessed by some person, at some time, indicated by the context.

If we suppose that this answer to our question about probabilities is the answer to our question about powers, some odd consequences do indeed result. For example, it would follow that A may say that B can do X, and could have done Y, and C may say that B cannot do X, and could not have done Y, and yet neither be contradicting the other. For the truth of A's assertion would be relative to A's knowledge, the truth of C's assertion, to C's knowledge. This would make a fine nonsense of all ascription of responsibility, which would be represented as indeed what the most rigorous metaphysical determinism asserts that it is, purely a measure of our ignorance. Another peculiar consequence would be that all attributions of power are elliptical.

Nevertheless, the theory that power consists in the possibility or probability of its exercise cannot be dismissed simply on these grounds, since very similar complaints can be made on behalf of the probability

[1] W. Kneale: *Probability and Induction*, p. 10; cf. Keynes, op. cit., p. 7.

statements we make 'in ordinary life'. For example, Keynes and his followers assert 'that to say that a probability is unknown ought to mean that it is unknown to us through lack of skill in arguing from given evidence', not, that is, through lack of evidence. But this is untenable. A claim about the expectation of life of some class of human beings is often given as a paradigm probability-statement, yet my present ignorance of the expectation of life of thirty-year-old Englishmen is in the main due to lack of evidence, rather than to lack of reasoning power or mathematical ability. It may well be that had I the evidence I still could not deduce the probability, but that would remain to be seen. The same question arises if I assert that the favourite in a horse-race has one chance in twelve of winning, while other people know that I have absolutely no knowledge of horses or horse-racing, but have simply been told incorrectly that there are twelve entries for this particular race. They would surely be right to regard my opinion as not only worthless, but false.

These counter-examples lead on to another. If I discuss with Jones the likelihood of our meeting Smith, our discussion may not take the form of an argument from given evidence, for throughout the discussion each of us may contribute further facts, as they come to mind. Certainly it is conceivable that we should from the start be in agreement over all the relevant evidence, and yet disagree over the probability of the meeting through a 'lack of skill in arguing from given evidence' of at least one of us. Yet even if we disagree over the evidence, we might still be correctly and truly described as discussing, and disagreeing about, the same probability – the likelihood of meeting Smith. The claim is that 'we commonly state probabilities in relation to all the knowledge we have at the time and therefore feel no need to specify the evidence'. Yet if each disputant specified his evidence he would almost invariably, at least at the beginning of the dispute, prove to have a different body of knowledge from the other. Accordingly there would initially be no contradiction. The disputants would not even know at first whether they were disagreeing: they would be like two children shouting 'He did', 'He didn't', but meaning different things.

These considerations may not count against the very vague principle that probability is relative to evidence, but they do count against the

Keynesian interpretation of this principle. Fortunately a different interpretation can be given. That is that these 'everyday' statements are not elliptical, because they are relative not to the body of knowledge actually possessed by someone or other, but to the body of evidence that is or was *available*. The same probability is being discussed as long as the evidence brought to bear by either side may rightly be said to have been available throughout the dispute. But a new question arises when evidence that was not so available comes under consideration. For example, in an argument about the chances of a Democratic victory in the American election, each disputant may not only introduce into the discussion, in support of his estimate, information that he already had but that he had not at first mentioned or, perhaps, remembered, but he may even refer for further information to sources such as history books or newspapers, without going beyond the evidence available from the start, and so without the subject of the discussion becoming a new and different probability. An unexpected call from New York, on the other hand, or the arrival of the evening papers, may create the sort of situation in which we might reasonably say that a fresh probability has come to be discussed. But there is no reason for regarding the available evidence as something that should or even could be stated in full, and certainly none for taking such a statement of evidence as a *part* of the proposition originally in dispute. And surely it is unacceptable that 'The Democrats will probably win' is normally elliptical, that something must be added if the sense of the utterance is to be completely expressed. It would be a very odd request, to ask that the speaker should state what he means in full. On my account, nothing has been left unsaid, for although the verification of the assertion requires that we determine what evidence was available to the speaker and how far this evidence supported the prediction that the Democrats would win, neither of these things need be determined in order to understand the assertion. If it is right to say that the probability-statement includes a reference to the available evidence, then it includes only an oblique, unspecific, determinable reference, which may be compared to the reference made to the number of leaves on a tree, when we are told that it is equal to the number of students in a college. In order to verify this statement we may need to count leaves and students, but not in order to understand it.

This theory may be illustrated from the discussions of probabilities that often arise in the lawcourts. For example, damages are recoverable for breach of contract, roughly speaking, if there was a likelihood of their resulting from the breach: i.e. if they 'may reasonably be supposed to have been in the contemplation of the parties at the time they made the contract, as the probable result of the breach of it' (*Anson's Law of Contract*, 20th ed., 1945, p. 366a). Cases illustrate that 'the probable result' is what was at all likely, relatively to the evidence *available* to the contracting parties, not, of course, to what they actually knew. For while there are some things that it would be unreasonable to expect contractors to know, many know less than a man in their position may reasonably be expected to know. The concept of negligence raises the same point. In one case (*Baker* v. *Hopkins*: (1959) 1 W.L.R. 966), a firm undertook to clean out a well. Under the supervision of the managing director, a pump was set up half-way down, in order to remove water, and was allowed to run for a while. Next morning the managing director, knowing that some fumes had been produced, told his men not to go down before he arrived, but without explaining the nature of the danger. He was delayed, and unfortunately two workmen did go down, and were overcome. Their deaths were held a probable and foreseeable result of 'a hazardous and dangerous method of operations'. Yet it was quite plain that the managing director was unaware of the probable consequences of his method of working, since it was liable to fill the well with deadly fumes for weeks. A 'foreseeable' result, to use the preferred legal term, is one that might reasonably be expected to have been foreseen, not in the light of the actual and perhaps unduly limited body of knowledge of a particular person or set of people, but in the light of the evidence that someone might reasonably be expected to have on call in the circumstances.

The defence of a mistaken prediction made in the past will constitute a justification of the claim that what was predicted was at any rate probable or possible. A past prediction is not defensible if whoever made it neglected to take into account all the available evidence. Similarly, if we are to assess a past probability claim, we must look beyond the evidence on which it was actually grounded, and consider rather what evidence was available at the time and in the circumstances in question.

As it has often been remarked, the verification of probability statements is closely associated with the justification of action. To justify the act of carrying an umbrella, we may need to show that on Friday it was probable that it would rain on Saturday. Of course, more than this may be required, since it is always debatable whether it would have been a bad thing to get wet on some occasion, or whether the risk of getting wet was not offset by the advantages of walking unimpeded. But it would be absurd to deny in general that probabilities should be taken into account when contemplating action. The Keynesian doctrine, however, leaves it open whether it is always rational to be guided in one's actions by what is probable. Certainly we are left with the question of which 'probability relation' is the important one. It might be argued in Keynes' defence that the truism that the rational agent takes probabilities into account means that it is rational to act on any probability that is relative to our complete knowledge. But this is inadequate, for it may be very foolish to enter on any course of action to which a particular question of probability is relevant without first obtaining further information, beyond what one possesses at the moment. As Keynes himself admits, to the maxim that we must take into account all the evidence we have, should be added Locke's maxim that we should keep ourselves as well informed as possible. The present account differs from that of Keynes in that it recognises that both these maxims are incorporated in the meaning of the probability-statement: to be as well informed as possible is to have a grasp of the available evidence. Consequently we do not require his supplementary explanation of the intuitively apparent relevance of probabilities to the justification of action.

The great advantage of the Keynesian theory over a theory like Hume's, is that it allows that questions of probability are objective, and not a matter of how one person feels. This advantage is not, of course, being lost in my account. It might be said that an acceptance of the objectivity of probabilities is being reinforced, in that they are seen not to be relative simply to what one person knows, or imagines that he knows.

The Keynesian theory plunges all probability into the realm of the universal and timeless. No claim that something is probable, certain or epistemically possible is allowed to have any more particularity than any logical relation holding between grounds and conclusion of an argument. No further information about the particular case in question is supposed to be relevant to the justification of any such claim, since the addition of this information would, it is held, make the claim a different one. Yet certainly a distinction is intuitively obvious between a particular or singular statement, e.g. that it is likely to rain this afternoon, or that this die will probably fall six uppermost, and, on the other hand, a general or universal statement, e.g. that rain is likely after a red morning sky, or that there is one chance in six that a die should fall with a six uppermost. It should be recognised that further information about the particular case may always be relevant to the verification of particular statements, since such information may always be part of the available evidence or, for that matter, may be of relevance in judging evidence available in the past.

Particularity is also at stake in our interpretation of cases of false evidence. Someone makes the assertion that an event X is likely, and tells us that he bases it on his knowledge that A, B, C and D are present, but not E, and on his experience over a large and varied range of instances, that under conditions like these, an event appropriately like X has nearly always occurred. According to the doctrine that his original claim was elliptical, it seems that we can say without any acquaintance with the particulars of the case that his claim was true, i.e. that X is, or was, likely. It requires no very great skill in arguing from given evidence to conclude that his premises do to a high degree support the conclusion that X will occur. Yet is it *therefore* the case that his claim was true? For we may suppose not only that he has overlooked some obvious factor, but also that his belief that A, B and C were present is mistaken, or that he dreamed all his previous 'experience'. This surely would be relevant. Consequently, although there may be nothing wrong with his skill in arguing from his premises or, as Keynes calls them, his hypotheses, his claim may be false. This question is begged when it is said that such probability-claims are relative to the speaker's knowledge, when presumably all that can be meant is that they are relative to what he thinks he knows. Neither explanation is correct. As the law recognises, what matters is what it is reasonable to expect him to know.

It is not to be supposed that the somewhat vague principles that probability is relative to the available evidence, and that what was probable is what it might reasonably be expected of someone to have anticipated, are likely to be of very much help in *answering* the kind of probability-question under discussion, even if similar principles are in fact sometimes employed in courts of law. These principles are intended only to help in making clearer the nature of such questions.

There are, moreover, minor complications which would need more discussion in a fuller account than ours. For example, we have criticised Keynes for making it virtually impossible for two people engaged on a question of probability to be debating the same thing, but it might be said that we ourselves have made it impossible for an expert and a layman to debate the same probability. For in general certain evidence is available to, say, a professional meteorologist that is not available to the layman. Yet if a group of people are arguing about the probability of rain that day, it seems odd to suggest that a professional meteorologist among them is debarred from giving his more informed opinion on the identical subject. Perhaps this case can be met by the point that a group of people engaged on the same question can be regarded as one person, in that what is a reason for one must be a reason for all. When the issue is a probability, information available to one can be regarded as available to all. And in fact the expert's special knowledge *is* available to the laymen in the group, as with any information that can be pooled. On the other hand, it would be quite artificial to argue that what each man actually knows, the group 'as a whole' also knows.[1]

4. SOME MORE THEORIES ABOUT PERSONAL POWER

We are now in a position to proceed with our task of sorting out the kinds of possibility, and to describe more accurately the relationship between relative possibility and possibility for choice. It will readily be

[1] Even this would hardly make the Keynesian account compatible with the natural interpretation of this case: since even to know what question is under discussion, we must, according to Keynes, know what the evidence is. But perhaps no individual knows what the group as a whole knows.

seen that, although the identification of the two is not quite as implausible on a correct account of relative possibility as it would be on the commonly accepted view, there are still powerful objections to it.

The sentence 'It is possible that Smith will call' is not characteristically elliptical nor indefinitely ambiguous as Keynes would have it, but it is still logically ambivalent in a peculiar way, in that the statement expressed by it on any particular occasion of its use depends for its identity, and so for its truth-value, on more than the usual considerations. It is a philosophical commonplace that the proposition expressed by a sentence may depend for its identity on more than the sense of the sentence. The proposition expressed by 'I am a descendant of the man in the iron mask' will be different, even though the sentence is used with the same sense or meaning, depending on the reference of 'I' and of 'the man in the iron mask'. But the truth-value, and so the identity, of the proposition 'It is probable, or possible, that I am descended from the man in the iron mask' depends on more than its sense and the reference of the pronoun and definite description, since it depends on the circumstances of the speaker, i.e. on what he is in a position to know. It is just this peculiarity that is marked by the principle that probability is 'relative', and it is simply odd that those who have popularised the principle have tried to explain away the peculiarity by the doctrine that probability-statements are elliptical. Be that as it may, the statement that it is possible *for* Smith to call obviously does not possess this peculiarity.

The difference is, indeed, forcefully illustrated by the very little that the identification of non-relative with relative possibility could achieve towards mitigating the objectionable paradoxes of metaphysical determinism. It is true that a way compatible with scientific determinism would be open for a rebuttal of the metaphysical determinist's taunt that every ascription of the power to do otherwise is a *mistake* made in ignorance of causes. But the equation of the power of choice between alternative possibilities with the co-existence of the possibility that an action will or would be performed and the possibility that it will or would not be performed, provides no defence in itself against the characteristic and disturbing claim that if we knew all the causes from which we could infer with certainty that something will be done, then we would also know enough to prove that the agent could not do otherwise.

In other words, to set the determinist aside for a moment, the equation is open to the simple objection that, surely, if it is certain that Smith will not go to the meeting, it does not follow that he cannot go, but it is perfectly conceivable that he could. What is more, it may now be uncertain whether he will go (i.e. possible that he will and possible that he will not), even if, as perhaps we shall come to learn, he is actually unable to go. To take another example, it may have been possible in the morning that we should cross a certain bridge in the evening, even if the bridge was then already down, and we find out in the evening, when we get there, that it has not been possible for anyone to cross for a week, and will not be for another week. Consequently 'possibility for' neither entails nor is entailed by 'possibility that'.

In spite of this, it is a popular move to attach the 'freedom' of an agent to uncertainty of some kind about what he will do. There is some excuse for this, since determinists not infrequently put their argument in terms of the theoretical predictability of actions, which is supposed to be incompatible with the possibility of doing otherwise. But determinists are also sometimes explicit that they regard predictability as important only as a mark of the causation of human action, and that their argument really hangs on the presumed fact of causation. Nevertheless some anti-determinists, while they are not prepared to embrace the traditional doctrine of indeterminism and the mysterious gap in causality, hold that, whether or not everything is caused, a proof of the impossibility of predicting an action with certainty can be given that will *ipso facto* prove, and explain, freewill and possibility for choice.

For example, Wittgenstein, in the *Tractatus Logico-philosophicus*, makes the assertion that 'The freedom of the will consists in the fact that future actions cannot be known now. We could only know them if causality were an inner necessity, like that of logical deduction.' He is here evidently falling in with a view common enough among writers on induction and probability, namely that nothing in the future is ever certain but is only at best probable, which is held on the Humean ground that it is always logically conceivable, and therefore possible, that the most secure of predictions should turn out false. A hypothesis is only certain in relation to a body of evidence, it is held, if it is deducible from it. If it is logically possible for a statement to be false and a set of evidential statements to be true, then the statement is not certain in relation to the set of statements. Thus it would follow that no statement about the future could ever be certain in relation to the evidence available at present, i.e. could ever be certain.

Wittgenstein's claim not only fails even to begin to give a satisfactory explanation of the freedom of the will, but also relies on an objectionable scepticism. To take the latter point first, it is a mistake to represent logical certainty as the upper limit of the range of degrees of empirical probability, a limit that, for good or ill, cannot be reached so far as the future is concerned. We have seen that the statement that it will probably rain is a contingent, empirical statement relative to the available evidence. It is not an acceptable view that the statement that it will certainly rain is so different as to be always and necessarily false, nor that the statement that it will possibly rain is always and necessarily true. Anyone who supposes that when we make relative possibility-statements about the future we mean something trivially true of all self-consistent predictions, is likely to have confused relative with logical possibility.

Yet apart from the unacceptability of the notion that the future never is nor could be certain, the supposition that in this consists the freedom of the will only seems to make sense if it is taken to be the further suggestion that possibility for choice can be identified with this possibility that applies to every prediction; and that a man's power to pursue either of two alternative courses of action consists in the logical possibility, if he does the one, that he should have done the other. Such a power would be singularly unrestricted, and wider, as it seems unnecessary to point out, than the power of choice would ever reasonably be supposed to be. This view, then, confuses not only logical and relative possibility, but also relative possibility and possibility for choice. One of two things to be said in its favour is that this dual confusion avoids making possibility for choice relative to evidence. The other is that, *given* the mistaken notion that certainty involves deducibility from the available evidence, it is very likely better to say that the future cannot be known for certain, than that the future could be deduced from the available evidence.

Very similar criticisms can be made of much more detailed arguments that have been taken as important and even as decisive contributions to the freewill controversy. It has been argued, for example, that since every observer is liable to have some effect on what he is observing, and as no observer could take fully into account in his calculations the effect he is at the moment having, then no certain prediction is possible, since some of the evidence requisite for certainty is necessarily unavailable.[1] If this argument proved anything, it would prove too much: even, presumably, that it is possible that the man at whom I am gazing through my window will turn into a bluebottle and fly away. But in any case this general scepticism about the future would hardly help to explain possibility for choice, which is at least sometimes undoubtedly lacking.

Another line of argument seems more pertinent. Its conclusion is that, even if scientific determinism is true and most events are predictable, human actions are unpredictable or uncertain in a special way that will explain what is meant when it is said that an agent could have done otherwise. The reasons given for ascribing this unpredictability raise complex issues which largely go beyond the scope of this book, although we shall return to some of them. At present I shall be concerned simply with the suggestion that 'possibility for' can be identified with, and explained as, a 'possibility that'.

One argument is that it is logically impossible that an agent should know for certain what he is going to do before he decides to do it, and that consequently where there is a decision between possibilities there is, *ipso facto*, uncertainty. Now it does seem absurd to suppose that a man should sit down and predict his own decision just before he makes it ('wringing his hands' if he did not like the decision, to use a phrase of the determinist Schopenhauer), on the basis, say, of his character, his present brain activity, his previous decisions in such circumstances or the like. It is sometimes suggested that this is because he would never be able to catch up on the evidence required for such a prediction, since it must include the fact that he is now making a prediction based on such and such evidence.[2] But this explanation would fail to

[1] *v.* K. R. Popper: 'Indeterminism in Quantum Physics', *British Journal for the Philosophy of Science*, Vol. I, nos 2 and 3. Popper himself seems to be concerned to refute scientific determinism, but he has been taken to have conclusively refuted metaphysical determinism (by, e.g., M. Cranston, in *Freedom: A New Analysis*).
[2] Cf. Ryle: *Concept of Mind*, p. 197 (quoted with approval by Popper, op. cit.).

discriminate between occasions when the agent has a choice and other occasions, since it would presumably apply to all his predictions involving himself. In any case it misses the real point, since it would not explain the undoubted queerness of the suggestion that a man should set about predicting his action even on the basis of the *available* evidence of his own character and so on, when a decision has to be made. Another reason offered, however, is that for a man to recognise that he is in a position to deliberate and to decide, he must regard the outcome of the decision as uncertain until it is actually made. If he is really to deliberate, the result of his deliberation cannot be a foregone conclusion as far as he himself is concerned: 'In *this* sense he is bound to recognise that he *may* decide in favour either of one alternative or the other.'[1] This suggestion is put forward as an explanation of the meaning of the statement that a man *could* do either of alternatives.

Now the reason why it is impossible that someone should foretell which piece of cake he will the next moment choose from the plate before actually deciding to take it seems to be this: whether or not he has any grounds for his prediction and whatever he takes them to be, it will always be open to him to falsify it by taking a different piece, so that belief in the assertion constitutes a decision not to do so, i.e. an actual choice. Whatever the result of his calculations, he is still faced with the decision whether to do what it foretells. A man who knows what he is going to do is, in general, a man who has made up his mind what he is going to do. Consequently any attempt on his part to support or justify his prediction – except in the way in which one can justify an intention or an action – will have an air of unreality or 'logical oddity', to use a recently popular expression. More plausible cases of the prediction of one's own choice before making it can be constructed if we suppose a longer period of time to elapse between prediction and choice, but very often even these carry a special implication of acceptance or of helplessness, as when I do not want a new tie but I know that I shall be persuaded to buy one. If there is no question of alternative possibilities and choice, however, there is

---

[1] A. K. Stout: 'Freewill and Responsibility', *P.A.S.*, vol. 37. *v.* also D. M. MacKay: 'On the Logical Indeterminacy of a Free Choice', *Mind*, 1960 (especially sections 6 and 7). Perhaps Moore had something similar in mind in the passage quoted above, p. 14. cf. S. Hampshire: *Thought and Action*, Ch. 2.

nothing strange in the notion of a man predicting on the basis of past experience what he will do or what will happen to him, in much the same way as he would predict the weather. If a master in control of his vessel tells us where we shall land and we take him to be announcing his decision, it would be inappropriate to ask him for his evidence for it, although we might ask for his evidence that he can implement it. It would not be inappropriate to ask for his evidence if we knew that the vessel was out of his control.

Yet can we extract from all this a 'sense' of *can* or *may* which would be acceptable as an explanation of the power to do either of two alternatives? It seems not. For one thing, the strangeness of the supposition that a man should offer grounds for his prediction of what he is just about to do, so far from implying that, for him, it is necessarily uncertain what he will do, seems if anything to be connected with the fact that he has a special right to say with certainty what he is going to do, and is in a special position to know it, this right deriving not from privileged access to special evidence, but simply from his being the one who decides. In any case, there is no reason why, in making a choice, an agent should at any stage have to 'recognise that he *may* decide in favour either of one alternative or the other', as a single instance will confirm. If I am asked to join in a mail robbery I do not have to pass through a brief period of doubt about what I shall do before deciding to refuse. Yet it may none the less have been possible for me to accept, and the immediacy of my reaction provides no reason for doubting that it is a genuine case of a decision to reject a possible course of action.

Moreover, while it may be a tautology that someone who has not made up his mind between alternative possibilities is uncertain which he will choose, his power of choosing either course of action cannot be co-extensive with the possibility *that* he will choose it, for the reason that, even after he has made up his mind to reject an alternative, it may well nevertheless remain a possibility for choice. A final decision to live in Oxford rather than Woodstock may do away with all uncertainty, without making it any the less possible *for* the person concerned to move to Woodstock at any time. One writer expresses the view we are criticising, by saying that 'our "firm subjective conviction of freedom" ... is the entirely justifiable corollary of [the fact that] for us as agents, any purported prediction of our normal choices as "certain" is strictly *incredible*, and the key evidence for it *unformulable*' (D. M. MacKay, op. cit., p. 37). It would presumably follow that my firm conviction that I am living in Oxford of my own free will and continue to live here because I choose to, must be a corollary of an inability to believe that it is certain that I shall not suddenly move away. Unfortunately for this account I should agree with close acquaintances that it is certain that I shall remain for a time, even if my right to say so is not so much a function of evidence I possess, as their ground for saying so may be. Briefly, it is absurd to equate freedom of action with a state of indecision.

This subject has many interesting implications for philosophy. For example, the notion that I have a special right to say what I will do not deriving from the possession of special evidence, conflicts with the traditional conception that a prediction, to the extent that it is not supported by evidence and inductive reasoning, must be a blind guess; and this may lead to the view that the expression of an intention, or any prediction deriving from an intention, cannot be a genuine 'prediction' or statement about the future at all. Such a view will not survive a consideration of the logical relationship between one person's expression of intention, 'I will go', and another person's forecast, 'He will go', which is the same as that between two corresponding forecasts, such as 'I shall faint' and 'He will faint'. A similar but much more perplexing difficulty arises with respect to 'I will certainly go', 'I will probably go' and 'I will possibly go', which it befits us to notice in view of our discussion of probability and relative possibility. 'I will certainly go' seems, at least at first sight, to be related to the corresponding third person statement 'He will certainly go' as 'I will go' is related to 'He will go'. But how could 'I will certainly go', if it is an expression of intention, mean 'It is certain in relation to the available evidence that I shall go', in accordance with our suggestions above as to the meaning of 'He will certainly go'? It cannot simply be said that this is a special and merely emphatic use of 'certainly' not relative to evidence, since 'I will certainly go' does imply something about the available evidence, namely that it leaves no doubt that I *can* go or, at least, shall be able to go – in general, 'I will' implies 'I shall be able to' – and this is a claim that the agent can intelligibly be called on to support. Similarly the qualified expression of intention, 'I will probably go', implies at least 'I probably can go', which is not and could not be an expression of intention. The somewhat perplexing thing is that 'I certainly will go' and 'I probably will go' can hardly be taken to imply any more than this about the available evidence.

We shall not pursue this problem here. Our present purpose is simply to shew that whatever the philosophical interest of the topic of the prediction of one's own acts, the ability of a person to do an action in the circumstances cannot with any credibility be identified with, or explained by, any sort of possibility *that* he will do it. It is not even a necessary condition, still less a necessary and sufficient condition for my having a choice between different courses of action that it should be uncertain which I shall choose, whether to other people or to myself.

5. AN ANALOGY BETWEEN TWO KINDS OF POSSIBILITY

There is, then, no direct logical connection between
A. *It is possible that Smith will call tonight* and
B. *It is possible for Smith to call tonight*,
contrary to theories and suggestions often advanced. There is, however, an analogy between them.

It is likely that the popularity of the kind of theory discussed in the last section can be attributed, on the whole, simply to the central part that the notion of 'predictability' plays in the determinist dialectic, which naturally tends to promote the conflation of 'Can he?' with 'Might he?' But we should recognise that, logically unconnected as they are, A and B really are logically and epistemologically similar in some respects. Sometimes at least it is this analogy, rather than anything directly related to the freewill controversy, that has tempted philosophers to identify them.

These similarities are obvious, and need not detain us long. If we consider the relation of A and B to
C. *Smith will call tonight*
it will be evident that the denial of A and the denial of B are alike in implying the falsity of C. This platitudinous simplicity can appear to be disrupted by tense and other factors, which is why a time-reference has

been included in A and B. For example, 'Smith cannot call' (no time-reference) does not entail 'Smith will not call', which follows only from 'Smith will not be able to call'; 'Smith cannot call' entails only 'Smith is not calling', or perhaps the curious mongrel, 'Smith will not call now'. How does the time-reference make a difference? It might seem to do its work by limiting, and determining the tense of 'can', in so far as tonight might seem to be necessarily the only time at which Smith would be able to call-tonight. But in fact there is reason to regard the 'can' as present, since there is a point in saying that someone has the ability now to do something in the future. Someone may now, at noon, be able to go to the theatre tonight, although, in the event, he will be unable to go: for example, if it is necessary to buy a ticket before two o'clock. So perhaps we should say that the time-reference limits the infinitive, determining the act, rather than the ability, to a particular time, and that it is for this reason only that 'Smith cannot call tonight' entails 'Smith will not call tonight', although 'Smith cannot call' does not entail 'Smith will not call'.

Whatever the entertaining complications, it is beyond dispute that the principle that '*p is impossible*' entails '*Not p*' is in general applicable to both kinds of possibility. So too with the converse: if C is true, then both A and B are true.

The applicability of these principles to relative or epistemic possibility marks a familiar difference between possibility, impossibility and certainty on the one hand, and probability and improbability on the other. To know that an event was antecedently possible, that it was not certain that it would not happen, it is enough to know now that it actually happened: but present knowledge of the occurrence or non-occurrence of an event is never sufficient to determine its antecedent probability. That epistemic possibility-claims may be verified, and impossibility-claims and certainty-claims falsified, simply by the way things turn out, tends to disguise the fact that these assertions, like probability-statements, are relative to the available evidence; and, of course, to open the way for the sceptical paradoxes that nothing is antecedently certain and everything and anything is antecedently possible. But even when it is derived from *p* itself, we can still think of 'It was possible that *p*' as relative to the antecedently available evidence. From 'Smith called last night' we can deduce at least one, no doubt trivial, fact about the antecedently available evidence: that it did not completely rule out this event.

Another elementary similarity between A and B is that they are alike in not entailing C and not entailing Not-C either; a point that might be put by saying that both mention Smith's calling tonight without implying either that it will or that it will not take place. This again might seem too much of a platitude to be worth stating even in a book on philosophy, but it is perhaps at this level that we must look in order to find what different kinds of possibility have in common. In fact, as we have already seen, even this platitude has been denied, and it should be mentioned as a fundamental source of perplexity about possibility in general and consequently as a source of confusion between types of possibility. It is a source of perplexity in that it invites the question: what else can be said about an event or state of affairs, in respect of existence, but that it will occur or that it will not, that it is so or that it is not? It is a consequent source of confusion because a philosopher who understands how it is sometimes intelligible to mention an event, saying not that it will or that it will not occur but merely that it is possible, is liable to suppose that this explanation applies whenever we talk of possibilities as opposed to actualities. It is the programme of this book to demonstrate that there are a number of different explanations for different cases, i.e. that there are different kinds of possibility. We must try to understand them one by one.

This diagnosis *in vacuo* needs the support of examples. Hume is pretty evidently a case, but a more recent instance of the disease, which is also a case of confusion between *'possibility for'* and *'possibility that'* occurs in Ryle's *Concept of Mind* (p. 127). He writes: 'To say that something can be the case does not entail that it is the case, or that it is not the case, or, of course, that it is in suspense between being and not being the case, but only that there is no licence to infer from something else, specified or unspecified, to its not being the case.' Now of the statement that it was possible that it would rain today ('It could have rained'), it is fair enough to say that it is equivalent to the statement that there was no licence to infer from the available evidence that it would not rain. From this explanation it is easily understood how such a claim is not shown to be false or true by the fact of no rain, and yet how it does not refer, of course, to some state midway between raining and not raining. But this does not mean that the same kind of explanation can be extended to 'Fido can howl', an example which Ryle oddly interprets as licensing the hearer not to rely on Fido's silence. Indeed, Ryle explicitly makes this interpretation quite general, to cover all talk of powers and abilities, when he asserts that 'roughly, to say "can" is to say that it is not a certainty that something will not be the case'. He does have more to say about powers and capacities than this, and we shall have more to say about his other theories, but here at any rate he is offering the same kind of theory as Hume and Moore. And he is trying to deal with the same problem as both these philosophers: namely, why *power* should ever be distinguished from its *exercise*.

Some of what Wittgenstein says in the *Brown Book*, during his examination of 'the role the words "can" or "to be able" play in our language', also smacks strongly of Hume. For example, he imagines a tribe who bet on wrestlers, and who give reasons for their bets in terms descriptive of the physique, health, previous experience and training of the athletes. He continues:

> If a man of our tribe has lost his bet and upon this is chaffed or scolded he points out, possibly exaggerating, certain features of the man on whom he has laid his bet. One can imagine a discussion of pros and cons going on in this way: two people pointing out alternately certain features of the two competitors whose chances, as we should say, they are discussing; A pointing with a gesture to the great height of the one, B in answer to this shrugging his shoulders and pointing to the size of the other's biceps, and so on. I could easily add more details which would make us say that A and B are giving reasons for laying a bet on one person rather than on the other.
>
> ... We should in a case like that just described not be surprised if the language of the tribe contained what we should call expressions of degrees of belief, conviction, certainty... It is also easy to imagine that the people of our tribe accompany their betting by verbal expressions which we translate into 'I believe that so and so *can* beat so and so in wrestling', etc.' (I. 59.)

The language of this passage is certainly somewhat tentative, but its gist is the by now familiar suggestion that the statement that someone is able to do something is essentially like the statement that he will possibly do it, and that we shall better understand the former if we realise this. Wittgenstein's argument, like Hume's, brings out an affinity between 'possibility for' and 'possibility that' beyond the basic logical affinities that have so far been mentioned in this section. This further similarity is epistemological, and is perhaps difficult to put precisely, but, roughly speaking, it consists in the fact that, when our knowledge of the possibility of something is not derived simply from its actuality, then it can and must be derived from what Hume, in exactly this connection, calls 'experience and practice of the world', i.e. from knowledge of other situations like the one in question. This is so whether the possibility is a matter of likelihood or a matter of ability. But as we shall see, this common epistemological feature is highly misleading, unless we recognise that it leaves room for very great variety.

Such then is the general and obvious analogy between relative possibility and possibility for choice, which may serve both as an excuse for the surprisingly common philosophical error of identifying them, and as some explanation of how it is that the term 'possible' has a use in saying such irreducibly different things.

3
Probability and Natural Powers

1. INTRODUCTORY

It is now time to turn to the other kind of possibility mentioned at the beginning of Chapter 2, but not discussed there. There is a variety of directions from which to attack the subject of 'natural possibility', but I shall try to advance from ground already held, and begin by contrasting it with possibility relative to the available evidence. I shall then compare the two kinds of possibility with what are commonly held to be two kinds of probability. This will take us quite away from the topic of people and their choices and decisions, and we shall not return to it until Chapter 6.

2. THE RELATION BETWEEN EPISTEMIC AND NATURAL POSSIBILITY

We can say of an inanimate object not only that it might possibly do such and such, but also that it can or could do it. It is one thing to assert of an event that it is possible that it will occur, but another to claim that it could occur. For example, we can distinguish between the claim that it is possible *that* a rocket *will* reach Mars, and the claim that it is possible *for* a rocket *to* reach Mars. Unfortunately we might express the latter – to the detriment of any neat demarcation in this area between 'possibility that' and 'possibility for' – 'It is possible *that* a rocket *should* reach Mars.' At least, my ear tells me so. The more obvious logical differences between these claims are much the same as those between relative possibility and possibility for choice. The one kind of possibility-statement does not entail the other. The assertion that such a rocket *could* be built does not imply that there is any possibility that one *will* be built. So too it may be certain that a natural power will never be exercised. 'It is possible that this car will do 100 m.p.h., but it certainly will not' is self-contradictory, implying both that the available evidence does and that it does not rule out an event, but there is nothing wrong with 'This car is *capable* of doing 100 m.p.h., but it certainly will not.'

That the converse also holds, is only slightly, if at all, less evident. If I assert that it is possible that animals live on Mars, I shall not be shown to have spoken falsely simply by a later discovery that conditions there make life impossible, since my assertion is relative to the evidence now available to me. That is to say, my claim is logically compatible with the truth of the proposition that life on Mars is a natural impossibility. Similarly it may at one time have been possible that witches conjured spirits from the grave, or that lead would one day successfully be transmuted into gold, even though both, as we now believe, are in fact naturally impossible. It may be possible or even probable that Smith's brand-new racing car will average 100 m.p.h. in the race this afternoon, even though some unknown defect in its manufacture actually puts such a performance beyond its capacity.

The logical independence of a relative possibility from the corresponding natural possibility may be disguised by the fact that it would be odd and indeed logically objectionable to say 'It cannot do 100 m.p.h., but it is possible that it is doing 100.' But this oddity is to be explained without casting doubt on our principle of independence, or supposing some special logical connection between the two types of possibility. It derives simply from the principle that 'p is not possible' entails 'Not p', and the fact that it is odd to say 'It is possible (on the available evidence) that p, but not p.' It is odd to say 'It cannot do 100 m.p.h., but it is possible (or probable) that it now will', simply because it is odd to say what this entails, i.e. 'It will not now do 100 m.p.h., but it is possible (or probable) that it now will.' This last is odd not because it is self-contradictory – if it were then 'it is possible that p' would entail p, and Hume would be right to argue that if an event does not occur then it was never really possible or probable that it would – but for some other reason, which need not deeply concern us. Perhaps it is just because it is odd to assert something at the same time as one implies that there is not sufficient evidence for it, or that what evidence there is points the other way. In any case, all that we need to notice is that, just as 'It is probable that p' and, *a fortiori*, 'It is possible that p' do not rule out 'Not p', so 'This car might do 100 m.p.h.' does not rule out 'This car cannot do 100 m.p.h.' Of course, 'It is possible that it will do 100 m.p.h.' entails 'It is possible that it can do 100 m.p.h.', by simple application of 'p entails that p is possible' to the subordinate clause (i.e. (p is RP) entails [(p is NP) is RP].

This logical independence is corollary to the fact that the one kind of possibility is relative or 'epistemic', the other absolute or 'ontological'. It might help to make this distinction clearer to draw an analogy with *a priori* possibility. If, in defence of the efforts of those mathematicians who were so much concerned to find a way of geometrically reducing a circle to a square, we say that, after all, it was possible that they would succeed, we are not thereby committed to the view that it is logically possible to square the circle. Nor, of course, do we mean to imply that this logical impossibility might perhaps have been overcome in some way, but merely that those who believed that the circle could be squared are not entirely to be blamed for failing to anticipate the proof that it *is* a logical impossibility. The same sort of thing applies to non-logical possibilities, and to say that it was possible that the alchemists were right, or that it is possible that poltergeists exist, or possible that this rocket will reach Saturn, is to assert nothing about 'ontological' or 'absolute' natural possibilities or powers.

Hume, of course, is denying existence to just this distinction when he says explicitly that the power of any thing consists in the possibility or probability that it will be exercised. But to say that a thing *can* do something is to make no sort of conjecture that it will do it, or, for that matter, that it has done it or is doing it. This is not, of course, to deny that only in the light of what actually happens can natural possibility be assessed. Support for any empirical statement can only be drawn from what actually is the case. It is how this evidence counts that is of importance in a philosophical account of possibility. Any oversimplification of this will present a distorted picture of a whole class of statements. For example, Hume claims that 'an experiment in the past proves a possibility for the future' (*Treatise*, p. 135). He means, presumably, that if something has happened, then it follows that it is possible that it will happen again. Yet it is not hard to call to mind cases of something that has happened, but that will certainly never happen again. We can often be certain that history will not repeat itself. Even if some philosopher is so practised in doubting the future as really to believe it possible that a Roman Empire will rise again identical in every detail with the last, it is unlikely to be the fact that such a conjunction of events has actually occurred once before that influences his reasoning. An experiment in the past does prove a natural possibility, but not a 'possibility for the future'.

In Hume's defence, however, it may be pointed out that, together with the fact that it comprises all the available evidence, the fact that just such a small black cloud on the horizon has grown into a thunderstorm does prove the possibility that this one will do the same. If a die has sometimes fallen six uppermost, and if this is all that we can find out relevant to the prediction of its performance next time, then it is epistemically possible that it will fall six uppermost again, as well as ontologically possible that it should.

Here there is a positive logical connection between natural and relative possibility, since knowledge that an event of a particular kind is naturally possible can play the same logical part as knowledge of its past occurrence. If, for example, the question at issue is whether this body of water, in this kettle, may possibly boil, it may be very relevant to know that it could boil. It is true that knowledge of the water's potentialities is not sufficient, and we must also determine the likelihood of their actualisation. But if all we know about the particular situation is that this substance is water and that water can boil, and if this really is all the available evidence, then it follows that the water may possibly boil. The example is intensely artificial, and it is perhaps difficult to imagine any realistic case. Nevertheless the logical point is unaffected. It can be clumsily expressed by the principle:

[(p is NP) is all the available evidence relevant to p] entails (p is RP).

This principle is no doubt used remarkably seldom. Perhaps we reason in accordance with it – and even this is not necessarily at all the same thing as to use it – as we gaze apprehensively at a bomb, which, we are told, is capable of blowing us all sky-high. Of course there is no need to worry if it is certain not to go off, but if all we know is that it *could*, then it *might*. The chief and perhaps the only philosophical interest of the principle is that it suggests a further comparison and contrast between possibility and the concept of probability, which will enable us to relate our discussion to a well-trodden field in philosophy.

3. A CRITICISM OF THE DOCTRINE THAT 'PROBABLE' IS AMBIGUOUS

The doctrine that ordinary probability statements are elliptical, requiring completion by a clause specifying the evidence possessed by the speaker or someone else, very often goes hand in hand with another view, that there are two irreducibly distinct kinds of probability. A consideration of this view may help us to understand the relationship between 'relative' and 'absolute' possibility.

Carnap, for example, argues that there are two main *meanings* of the word 'probability', the two *concepts* being 'degree of confirmation', which he calls 'probability$_1$', and 'relative frequency in the long run', called by him 'probability$_2$'.[1] *Probability$_1$* is said to be a measure of the relationship of confirmation which may hold between two statements, the statement of the entire evidence for a hypothesis, and the hypothesis itself, i.e. 'an empirical statement not directly known to be true': for example, the relationship between a statement specifying the results of all known previous casts of this die and of other dice just like it, and the statement that the next throw with this die will be an ace. This relationship holds between propositions, is knowable *a priori* and is logical. *Probability$_2$*, on the other hand, is concerned with the relation between two properties or classes of things or events, etc.: in the example, 'The probability$_2$ of casting an ace with this die is $\frac{1}{6}$', the properties are that of being a throw with this die and that of being a throw resulting in an ace. This kind of probability statement is to be supported by statistics. Thus it is factual and empirical. There is no need to inquire here into the adequacy of Carnap's phrase 'relative frequency in the long run', so long as its use is intelligible.

Other writers make very similar claims. A favourite argument for the view that there are two quite different senses of the word 'probable' is that 'probable' and cognate expressions are reiterable within the same statement: it can be said that it is probable that the probability of heads

[1] In 'The Two Concepts of Probability', *Philosophy and Phenomenological Research*, 1944–5.

is ½, or *likely* that the *expectation* of life of a doctor of fifty is twelve years. In the one case, it is argued, we use the word *in* a generalisation to indicate that it asserts a proportional regularity or is a statistical generalisation: in the other case we use the word *about* a generalisation which may itself be a probability statement of the first kind.[1]

If we remember that those who advance the view that 'probable' has two senses, also as a rule hold that such a sentence as 'It will probably rain' must be regarded as elliptical, it will be clear that their distinction simply hinges on the familiar enough difference between two things that may count as giving a reason or mentioning evidence for a prediction or any hypothesis. If I am asked to justify a prediction that it will rain today and I simply reply that the sky was red this morning and, besides, the cattle are now lying down, I have undoubtedly given reasons, but such that experience is required to know that they are good reasons. Giving this kind of reason involves pointing out some feature of the situation, or further specifying it, and the reasons can be called 'specificatory' (after Urmson, op. cit.). If, however, I go on to list meteorological records, including, no doubt, reference to a majority of occasions on which conditions like these have been followed by rain, then experience is not required to know whether what I say, if it is true and other things are equal, constitutes a reason for my prediction. It is an *a priori* question whether Russell's chicken in *Problems of Philosophy*, which, if I remember rightly, has been fed every morning of its life but in the end runs up only to have its neck wrung, nevertheless had good reason to expect to be fed on its last morning too. Pure thought will tell us that it had very much better reason than if it had never been fed, but on the contrary, had been chased round the yard every day by a man with a cleaver. This kind of evidence may be called 'statistical'.

Correspondingly, if every statement, 'It is probable that p', is supposed to be elliptical and short for 'It is probable, in relation to evidence e, that p', then obviously a lot will depend on the kind of thing we use to replace the variable e. It has been suggested that the very meaning of 'probable' depends on it. We can agree at any rate that it will determine whether the probability-statement is empirical or *a priori*. But how, according to the doctrine that they are elliptical, are

[1] *v.*, e.g., J. O. Urmson: 'Two of the Senses of "probable"', *Analysis*, 1947–8.

we supposed to complete everyday probability statements, like 'It will probably rain today'? Are these elliptical 'probability$_1$' statements, or elliptical 'probability$_2$' statements? The view that they are elliptical certainly leaves us with this choice, and it is difficult to know how it should be determined. It seems that we can simply take our pick, depending on what we like to think has been left out. But the chief trouble is that, whichever we choose, we face paradox.

Since the elided portion of the statement is held to comprise the entire relevant knowledge of someone or other, it might seem reasonable to take it to be statistical, statistical evidence being in principle more complete than specificatory evidence alone. The notorious and surely unacceptable conclusion would follow, that the statement that it will probably rain is such that, if true, it logically could not have been false, and, if false, could not have been true, and that the question whether it will probably rain can and must be settled *a priori*. Besides, it can be very seldom that someone who asserts that it will probably rain can call to mind an appropriate set of statistics, not to speak of his already having it in mind. He is at any rate more likely to be able to give reasons of a 'specificatory' sort.

Let us take it, then, that this kind of assertion involves Carnap's 'probability$_2$', and that its 'understood' part is purely specificatory:[1] e.g. '... relative to the proposition that the sky was red this morning and the cows are lying down'. This theory is in line with our intuitions, and with common sense, at least to the extent that it allows the question whether it is probable that it will rain today to be an empirical question. But the theory still has the objectionable implication that this question is not about an impending state of the weather, and that the answer does not depend on the present state of the weather or of anything else. For it holds that the statement that rain is probable before nightfall simply asserts that something always provides reason for expecting rain before nightfall. Just what this is, is unfortunately concealed from us by the supposed ellipsis, but it would be something like a red sky in the morning. The paradoxical implication that all probability statements are general is openly accepted by some theorists, who claim that it is senseless to talk of the probability that a particular event, such as Napoleon's defeat, should occur or should have occurred. Napoleon

[1] Following, e.g., Kneale, op. cit.; *v.* especially Ch. I.

himself, or Waterloo, cannot figure in a probability statement; only, at best, anyone Napoleonic or anything Waterloolike.

My own account, given in the last chapter, is that the statements that it will probably rain today, that it was probable that Napoleon would win, and that the Theory of Relativity is probably correct, are not short for longer statements specifying relevant data of one kind or another, and, indeed, are not elliptical at all, although or, rather, because they *are* relative to the available evidence. The fact is that Carnap and other writers have failed to see that statements of the form '(In relation to the available evidence) it is probable that p', of which the portion in parentheses is redundant, are significantly different from statements of the form 'It is probable in relation to $e^1 - e^n$ that p', where $e^1 - e^n$ are actually specified data.[1] For the general question whether p would be confirmed or established by e, let e be 'statistical' or merely 'specificatory', is a different type of question from the question whether, going on what is available to us, we can confirm or establish p. Curiously enough, in view of the theories generally associated with the slogan that probability is relative to evidence, a reasonable way of marking the difference would be to say that whereas the answer to the second question is relative to, or depends upon the available evidence, the answer to the first is not relative to evidence at all, but is absolute and independent.

It might be said that we now have on our hands not two senses of 'probable' but three; and it is true that we have so far given recognition to three kinds of probability-statement:

1. Corresponding to Carnap's 'probability$_1$', where the evidence is actually specified as a part of the statement and is statistical: e.g. 'Given (only) the statistics $e^1 - e^n$ about doctors, the expectation of life of a doctor of fifty would be twelve years.' These statements are *a priori* and general.
2. Corresponding to 'probability$_2$', the evidence being specified as a part of the statement, and being purely specificatory: e.g., 'On the evidence (alone) that a creature has wings, the probability that it can fly is high.' Such statements are empirical and general.

[1] The two formulations are used indiscriminately by writers who are clearly unaware of the significance of their difference: v., e.g., Urmson, op. cit., pp. 191 and 193, and Kneale, op. cit., pp. 14 and 19.

3. Where no evidence is specified, the whole statement being relative to the available evidence: e.g., 'It will probably rain today', 'It was probable that Newtonian physics was correct.' Such statements may be either particular or general.

Yet are we to say that there are therefore three or even two different senses of 'probable' involved? I think that this account of the matter can be seen to be misconceived if we take an approach almost diametrically opposed to the orthodox one, thereby putting a conceptual horse back in front of his cart. The orthodox post-Keynesian approach is to plump for either (1) or (2) as the fundamental type of probability-statement, taking (3) to be explained as a special elliptical case of it; or to grant (1) and (2) separate but equal status, but still subordinating (3) to one or other of them. Let us, however, regard (3) as asserting that something is *really* probable, (1) and (2) being modified versions, modified by a subordinate clause which is somewhat analogous to a hypothetical clause. This is simply to recognise that 'probable' does after all mean something like 'fit to be believed' or, indeed, 'credible'. To say that, given e, then p would be credible is not to say that p is really credible. But neither is it to use the word 'credible' in any different sense from its normal sense in the categorical assertion. And so it is with 'probable'. Any differences in kind between our three 'types' of probability-statement are entirely explicable by the presence and nature of the subordinate clauses, a multiplication of senses of 'probable', or concepts of probability, being neither necessary nor in the least useful.

The relation between 'p is probable, relative to e' and 'p is (really) probable' is not unduly complex. The addition of a subordinate clause specifying exactly what is to be taken into account as 'evidence', transforms the statement into a principle that may be of use in answering primary questions as to whether something is really probable. A question as to the expectation of life of a doctor of fifty *given* certain statistics about doctors (a question that, as Keynes puts it, demands only skill in arguing from given evidence) is a purely theoretical question, and is of a kind likely to be asked very often, I should imagine, only in some actuarial text book. To concern oneself with doubts about the truth of the given 'evidence' or the method of acquiring it, or with hopes of acquiring more, as we might well do, if we were concerned with 'What is the expectation of life of a doctor of fifty, *really*?', would be to betray the same sort of misunderstanding of the question asked as is shewn by the schoolboy who rejects a mathematical problem about a bricklayer who lays 500 bricks per hour, on the grounds that no one can lay bricks so fast, or that his trade union would not allow it.

A question or statement is none the worse for being purely theoretical, of course. All that needs to be recognised is that probability-statements in general are not fundamentally or characteristically purely theoretical. Philosophers like Keynes who suppose that they are, have committed an interesting fallacy. It is true that in determining a probability there may come a stage after the available evidence has been empirically ascertained, when purely reflective thought is necessary, and is all that is necessary, in order to reach a conclusion; so that great 'skill in arguing from given evidence', and the mathematical principles proffered by statisticians and logicians, may be useful or even, let us grant, in many cases indispensable. Yet this is not to say that the question is itself an *a priori* question, or that it has become one. It is a common mistake to suppose in certain cases, of which probability is one, that because principles of logic or mathematics or other *a priori* principles are of use in answering a question, then the answer to that question is of the same type as the principles. On the contrary, the procedure adopted by an accountant, a physicist, a lawyer or anyone else may be purely reflective, involving not further empirical investigation, since all that is necessary or possible may already have been done, but the use of *a priori* principles; yet the question on which they continue to be engaged, such a question, say, as whether Smith and Son is solvent, whether Mercury obeys the laws of Newtonian physics, or whether the Sydney Harbour fire was foreseeable, may nevertheless be as factual or empirical as any question can be. Comparably we may prove that Socrates is mortal by means of the famous syllogism, but whether Socrates is mortal remains a matter of empirical fact. It is by its usefulness in answering questions of fact that logic can be seen to 'hook onto the world', to use a lively expression of Wittgenstein's. But there is a great difference between making use of an *a priori* principle and establishing an *a priori* principle; between the question whether Socrates really is mortal, and whether, given specified premisses, it would follow that Socrates is mortal; and between the question whether rain in the Sahara is really more probable in December than in June, and whether, assuming only certain specified statistics as evidence, rain there would be more probable in December than in June.

So too when e is simply specificatory, the statement that 'Given only e, p is probable' is a principle, this time empirical, that may be of use in determining whether p is probable. If we want to know whether rain is probable before nightfall tonight, it may be valuable to know that, in general, if the morning sky is red then rain before night is probable. But it is a mistake to try to identify these two bits of knowledge.

It is an elementary point that the way in which a probability principle has application to questions of real probability is not just like the way in which unqualified universal principles have application to particular questions of fact. 'All red morning skies are followed by rain before nightfall' together with 'This morning the sky was red' entails the proposition that there will be rain before nightfall, but 'The probability of a red morning sky being followed by rain is high' and 'This morning the sky was red' do not together entail that today rain is highly probable. For such a conclusion the further premiss is required that the minor premiss comprises all the available evidence about the present situation.[1] A related point brings out a difference between the subordinate clause in a probability principle and an ordinary hypothetical clause. 'If e, then p', together with e, entails p. But 'Relatively to e (given only, assuming only, that e), p would be probable', together with e does not entail that p is probable. Hence the significance of the 'only'.

In this connection we might notice a distinction that helps our case. There is a difference between a probability principle, e.g. the theoretical, text-book pronouncement, 'Given only that (relative to the

---

[1] There is, of course, a syllogism of a sort with precisely this conclusion: i.e. It is highly probable that all red morning skies are followed by rain. This morning the sky was red. Rain is highly probable today.

This provides a compelling argument against some forms of the 'two senses' doctrine, according to which the sense in which a general statement may be probable is different from the sense in which an event may be probable. But the occurrence of 'highly probable' in both premiss and conclusion of our syllogism proves that the sense is the same. Cp., e.g., Kneale: op. cit., especially Part IV and pp. 22 and 214.

evidence that ..., if all we can know is that ...) Mrs *A* has hung out her washing for the last six days, then it is probable that she will hang it out today', and a hypothetical primary or 'real' probability statement about a particular person, 'If Mrs Smith has hung out her washing for the last six days, it is probable that she will hang it out today.' The latter is relative to the available evidence about Mrs Smith (Is she a fundamentalist?), the day of the week (Is today Sunday?) and so on, even though it does not categorically assert that something is probable. It would seem impossible to account plausibly for this evident distinction on the orthodox view that ordinary probability statements are elliptical theoretical statements.

Although it has been necessary to go into a certain amount of detail in the discussion of probability, the better to question some current philosophical approaches, my purpose throughout has been to enable a comparison with possibility. Before I move on to complete this process of comparison, it should be acknowledged that many problems, some of them very general, remain in the metaphysics or, if preferred, 'semantics' of probability, not to speak of problems in the methodology of calculating probabilities. For example, there remains the vexed question of statements of intention, and the relation between Smith's assertion that he will probably resign and Jones' assertion that Smith probably will not resign. If Smith's qualified statement of intention is to count as a primary probability-statement, then perhaps the principle that such statements are 'relative to the available evidence' is of limited application, and cannot be as straightforwardly incorporated into the meaning of 'probable' as I may have suggested. An answer to this might have to wait on a reasonable sorting out of the notions of 'meaning', 'verification', 'justification', 'use', and so on, and a critique of popular philosophical arguments from one to another. The same applies to the question whether a special 'concept' of probability is required to explain the probability of *a priori* propositions; for example, the statement that Goldbach's Theorem is probably true.[1] But my basic contentions, the recognition that 'everyday' probability-statements are not elliptical but should be regarded as primary, and the

---

[1] 'True', indeed, is another word about which much the same questions arise. Briefly, it is a mistake to see a direct connection between the method of verification of '*p* is true' and the meaning of 'true'.

refusal to multiply senses of 'probable' implausibly and unnecessarily, are at least likely to facilitate a satisfactory solution to these and other problems.

4. A COMPARISON OF POSSIBILITY WITH PROBABILITY

In the last section I distinguished between three kinds of probability-statement, and it may throw some light on possibility and its relation to probability if we now consider how far the same classification can be applied to possibility.

The first two classes comprised what might be called 'closed' probability-statements, involving an assertion that something would be probable on an explicit, and exclusive, supposition. By 'exclusive' it is meant that nothing is to be taken into consideration but the supposition. Our chief interest in these assertions-on-a-supposition lay in the fact that philosophers have regarded one or other of them as being of fundamental importance in the metaphysics of probability, allowing them logical priority over the simple assertion that something is probable, full stop.

The first class comprised statements in which the exclusive supposition is statistical and which are verifiable *a priori*. We can construct just the same sort of possibility-statement, although it has little separate interest. 'In relation to $e^1 - e^n$, it would be possible that p', would be true if $e^1 - e^n$ would not constitute sufficient evidence to make 'Not p' certain. It is *a priori*, being concerned with the relation between all the premisses and the conclusion of a specifically limited inductive argument. It is not to be confused with the proposition that it is *logically* possible that $e^1 - e^n$ and p are both true (cf. p. 28 above).

The second class of probability-statements comprised those in which the integral supposition is 'specificatory'. Once again a simple conversion of 'probable' into 'possible' will result in an apparently straightforward parallel. From an example of the kind of statement Carnap has in mind when he talks of 'probability$_2$', we should get 'Given only that the morning sky was red, rain before nightfall is possible.' The two do seem to be closely alike, both being concerned with 'a relationship between general characteristics', and both being verifiable empirically. But of particular interest to us should be the fact that the latter is apparently what we have hitherto called a 'natural possibility' statement: it seems identical with 'It is possible for rain to follow a red morning sky.' In general, 'Given only that something is A, it is possible that it is B', construed as an empirical generalisation corresponding to Carnap's 'probability$_2$', seems to be identical with the proposition that it is possible for an A thing to be B.

Something entirely satisfactory would appear to follow, but also something not so satisfactory. In the first place, it would mean that we could explain natural possibility-statements without proliferating senses of 'possible' – for to talk of two senses of 'possible' or even of two concepts of possibility might seem to reduplicate the errors we have criticised in our discussion of probability. But the other, less acceptable consequence of treating possibility as entirely analogous to probability would be that 'absolute' or natural possibility would be seen as semantically subordinate to 'relative' or epistemic possibility. For as we have argued, this is the correct approach to probability. Such a conclusion, in the case of possibility, is intuitively objectionable, and our intuitions are not without foundation.

One difference that we have already noticed between possibility and probability, is that, whereas all that can be derived from a positive or negative probability-principle is another probability-statement, from a negative natural possibility-statement we can derive a proposition about actuality: 'p is not possible' entails 'Not p'. Natural and epistemic possibility-statements are therefore in a looser relationship than the corresponding probability-statements. But more than this point lies behind the feeling that natural possibility is not to be explained satisfactorily *via* epistemic possibility.

I have held that our second class of probability-statements will all be general, being concerned with a relationship between general characteristics. Here I am in agreement with most writers on probability. The point is that simply to include a 'this' in such a statement – 'Given only that *this* is A, it is probable that it is B' – is not to produce anything logically distinct from the general statement. The result would only achieve real particularity if, as in ordinary probability-statements, we were allowed to take into consideration indefinitely more about the situation than the property of being A – which, *ex hypothesi*, we are not. A contrast can be drawn with hypothetical statements, which some philosophers think must all be general, this time mistakenly. 'If anything is A, then it is B' no doubt entails 'If *this* were A, then it would be B', but is not entailed by it. The two statements, one general and one particular, are therefore logically distinct.

It is, then, a striking difference between this second class of probability-statements and what I have called natural possibility-statements that the latter may be irreducibly particular, so that we can significantly say that it is possible for *this* to go at 100 miles an hour. The difference is clearly presented in the contrast between

A. It is possible for an X thing to be Y.

(e.g., *a.* It is possible for a car to do 400 m.p.h. A car could do 400 m.p.h.) and

B. It is possible for any X thing to be Y.

(e.g., *b.* It is possible for any car to do 20 m.p.h. All cars can do 20 m.p.h.)

At first glance A and B may seem to be identical, but *a*, together with *c*. This is a car.

does not entail that this can do 400 m.p.h., while *b* and *c* together do entail the particular proposition that this can do 20 m.p.h. There is no parallel contrast to be drawn among probability statements and there is no parallel to 'This can do 20 m.p.h.' We do not talk of a thing's probabilities as we talk of its powers, its potentialities or, indeed, its possibilities. Why not?

This question raises important issues, which I shall approach from different directions in the chapters that follow. The answer is related to the explanation of the logical feature of 'ontological' possibility and power with which I have been concerned: a possibility or potentiality may exist that we know will not be actualised. For example, whether a thing 'does an action' or suffers a change of some specific sort will at least very often depend on the circumstances in which it is placed, as well as on itself or its own nature. Just because the conditions are such that the potentiality is not in fact actualised, it does not cease to be a potentiality. Thus we can, without a whiff of contradiction, categorically assert the possibility of the action while admitting that its non-performance is certain. But sense could hardly be given to the notion of a 'probability' of doing an action 'possessed' by a thing, and part of its nature, such that, from our knowledge of the circumstances, we could be certain that it would never be actualised. There is no way of saying, unless a modifying clause is included such as a 'given only ...' or an 'if ...' clause, that x's doing a is probable, without implying that there are good grounds for a prediction that x will do a: i.e., without making an 'epistemic' statement relative to the available evidence, whether evidence of the nature of x or evidence of x's circumstances. Taken in one way, the assertion that x's doing a is a possibility carries a similar 'epistemic' implication, but taken as a natural possibility-statement it does not.

The dichotomy between a thing's 'nature' and its circumstances, between its intrinsic and its extrinsic properties, requires much further explanation and will be seen to be fundamental to an understanding of potentiality. 'Nature' is not the same as 'identity', although they are sometimes confused. A thing may lose or acquire powers, like other properties, without a change of identity, but, unlike some other properties, not without a change in its nature.

The difference between particular potentialities and general possibilities might be expounded as follows. The general claim that it is possible for an A thing to be B asserts that there is not a universal connection between two properties, being A and being not-B. Nothing is implied about any particular thing. Now although the ascription of a power to a thing is *like* the general possibility-claim, it cannot be represented as if it were about a relation between properties, unless we are prepared to count as a property of something the 'property' of being the thing that it is, having the nature that it has, i.e. a 'property' defined by reference to its possessor. Since it is left open what the nature of the thing actually is, and since this question is irreducibly about a particular, the question whether the thing possesses some power is also irreducibly particular. We shall discover that this account is not so simple as it may sound, but at least it cannot be disguised that a possibility-statement can be made, without any modifying clause, that is informative about a particular and that is not any kind of prediction or other sort of conjecture about the actual course of events. This is to take at least two steps from the 'epistemic' world of probability.

All this is not surprising and is not meant to be, since it is a first attempt to justify and explain intuitions that have sometimes been given short shrift. In fact, anyone at all sensitive to the linguistic models we employ should feel suspicious of a theory that totally assimilates probability and possibility. The words 'probable' and 'possible' may sometimes come so close as to be virtually interchangeable. Few would quibble, in most contexts, between 'equally probable' and 'equally possible'. But the words have arrived at this synonymy from very different directions.

'Probable', with its root notion of approval, is obviously quite at home in the sphere of appraisal of beliefs and hypotheses in the light of their justification. The same applies to 'likely', which springs from the notion of comparison with the truth, or with fact. 'Possible', on the other hand, comes not from the sphere of theorising, judging and appraising beliefs, but originated in the notion of a powerful man – the same root, we are told, as 'despot'. So *'possum'* came to mean, in general, to be able to *do* things, and the adjective 'possible', to refer to what may be *done*. Similarly, Austin's ubiquitous frog in the philosophical beer-mug, 'can', has blown itself up from the notion of knowing how to *do* things. Etymology may be no substitute for philosophical argument, but perhaps even an amateurish etymological interest will help our philosophical understanding of possibility if it can bring us, for a moment, to think of 'It is possible that it will rain' or 'He could be alive' as an exotic figure of speech, which 'It is probable that it will rain' is certainly not. We should not be surprised, therefore, if 'possible' may be used where 'probable' cannot follow.

4
Some Unobservable Properties

1. INTRODUCTORY

An attempt must now be made to understand some epistemological problems that have given rise to unacceptable theories about the nature of potentiality, theories that all tend to terminate in metaphysical determinism. I shall suggest that these problems necessarily cannot be instantly dispelled by the 'analysis' of possibility-statements into something equivalent but unproblematical: the feature of possibility-statements that underlies them is irreducible. Nevertheless an analysis or theory will be offered, which, it is hoped, will give birth to an understanding of the source of the traditional difficulties, even if this proves a laborious rather than Caesarean procedure.

I shall discuss some very general complaints that may be brought against my theory, but its chief defence in the face of such criticism will be in its contribution, in later chapters, towards solving some further puzzles about power and possibility that are not overtly epistemological. This clarification, for which the present chapter is mainly preparatory, will include a treatment of possibility for choice, and the main part of my refutation of metaphysical determinism.

2. CERTAINTY, NECESSITY AND HUME

The difference between 'epistemic' or relative possibility and 'ontological' or natural possibility corresponds to the difference between certainty and necessity. The statement that it is possible that it will rain is equivalent to the statement that it is not certain that it will not rain, while the statement that it is possible for it to rain on the day following a red sunset is the same as the statement that the day after a red sunset is not necessarily not a rainy one. Certainty is relative to the available evidence, necessity is not. Neither implies the other. In case it should be thought, as it often is, that certainty is proof of necessity, we should consider what it would normally mean to say, for example, that a particular car *necessarily* travels at low speeds: namely, that it is incapable of travelling at other than low speeds. Now the statement that it is *certain* that a car travels, or will travel, at low speeds, does not imply that it is capable of travelling only at low speeds. The determinist will disagree, and this issue will receive very full discussion.

The notion of natural necessity is the subject of a great deal of controversy among philosophers. It is often suggested that all talk of non-logical necessity is confused and wrong, and it is orthodox among 'empiricist' philosophers to take a less tolerant attitude towards it than towards talk of possibility and power. Hume, on the other hand, the greatest of the Empiricists, succeeds in maintaining in at least much of what he says about power and necessity an admirable impartiality and consistency of approach. For example, we have seen that on one occasion at least he identifies power with the possibility that it will be exercised, and so we need not be surprised that he also gives the same account of necessity as of certainty. Although his discussion of these concepts must be among the very best-known of philosophical texts in English, it may advance our present purposes if we review some aspects of it.

Hume's earlier mentions of power in the *Treatise* are subordinate to his concern with necessity and causality. His treatment of causality, as it will be wearisome to repeat, is central to his attack on what is generally known as a 'Rationalist' epistemology. Given the differences between one Rationalist and another, 'The Rationalist' is certainly a somewhat shadowy figure. We can perhaps define Hume's target by reference to an ideal of explanation and understanding, which is supposed to be attainable at least in principle, although perhaps only by God, that presupposes that explaining and understanding an event is just like explaining and understanding a geometrical theorem. The relation between any real cause and its effect is represented as of the same kind as the relation between, say, the squareness of a figure and the incommensurability of its diagonals with its sides. It is therefore supposed that, given a situation in which the presence of a factor X can be explained by the presence of Y, we ought to be able to 'see' or realise this connection between X and Y simply from an acquaintance with the situation in isolation and from reflection upon it. Correspondingly it is supposed that, ideally at least, we should be able to infer all the consequences of a state of affairs simply from an acquaintance with it. If we cannot do so, then this is because we are not well enough acquainted with it, or else lack the capacity for the requisite reflection. In general, the Rationalist is prepared to condemn human cognitive capacities as feeble, in so far as he recognises that physical science fails to come up to his quasi-mathematical ideal.

Hume, on the other hand, rightly prefers the view that there is no ideal possibility of the explanation of an event, or of the justification of an inference from one event to another, that does not depend on reference to other situations beyond the one actually in question; i.e., that is not essentially inductive. It is true that he is inclined to deny that inductive inference and explanation is rational or can lead to real knowledge. In this respect he may not seem to differ much from Spinoza who contemptuously classified it as a function of the imagination. Yet Hume's great achievement is to have undermined the view that there might be a superior method of explanation or of inference from one fact to another; in particular, the view that the explanation of an event or thing might be as self-evident, to a being suitably endowed, as the truth of a simple proposition of logic. His scepticism consists in the fact that, having cast off the Rationalist illusion that such a superior or more conclusive method is logically possible, he has not entirely cast off the Rationalist's contempt for the only logically possible method. On the other hand, he is prepared to accept it as the way we think, and the only way to think effectively.

Hume's fundamental insight is expressed in his principle that

> the inference we draw from cause to effect, is not derived merely from a survey of these particular objects, and from such a penetration into their essences as may discover the dependence of the one upon the other. There is no object, which implies the existence of any other if we consider these objects in themselves and never look beyond the ideas we form of them [i.e., *scil.*, of their sensible

properties]. Such an inference would amount to knowledge, and would imply the absolute contradiction and impossibility of conceiving anything different. (Bk I, Pt III, Sect. VI.)

It is in relation to this principle that his treatment of power, like his treatment of necessity and certainty, although inadequate, incorrect and unclear, can yet be seen as a positively valuable contribution to an understanding of understanding and inference. For one line of objection to his principle, which he evidently thinks it important to rebut, is the objection that it is not impossible to deduce from the intrinsic properties of an event or state of affairs that some other will follow it, for the reason that it is possible so to deduce the existence of any effect from the existence of the cause and the necessary connection linking cause to effect, or from the existence of the power of the cause to produce the effect.

Hume's response is to demonstrate that a necessary connection is itself not a relation that can be recognised if we 'never look beyond' our experience of the particular event or state of affairs in question. Knowledge that something happens necessarily is inconceivable without the same sort of wider experience as is required to justify the corresponding inference. Consequently it is a misconception that an awareness of the presence of a necessary connection would obviate, for us or for God, the need to look beyond the single occasion in order to justify an inference or explanation. This is the valid point that Hume makes about necessity, although in the course of making it he is led to misrepresent necessity and certainty, as well as power and possibility, in other respects.

The argument that we can deduce the occurrence of a future event from the existence of the *power* of an agent to produce it, an argument that might seem to identify power with necessity, is rather curious, since it is clearly impossible to deduce that an event will happen simply from the fact that something is capable of making it happen. *p is possible* does not entail *p*.[1] But Hume does not bring this objection. He is

---

[1] The overtly realist conception of power criticised by Hume is not, of course, an essential or even characteristic feature of classical Rationalism. Descartes, who associated the concept with Scholastic pseudo-explanations, would have been particularly scornful of an argument that Hume attributes to the opposition: 'The past production implies a power: The power implies a new production: And the

content to treat power in much the same way as necessity, resting his argument on the point that, unless the 'agent' actually acts, we cannot tell whether the power is present from a consideration of the agent alone. The case in which the power is actually exercised, and so presumably *can* be known to be present from the particular case alone, does not count against the general claim about inference, which is that no inference *to* the effect is possible from the cause considered in isolation from experience of similar instances (cf. *Treatise*, p. 91). The conception of a power as a quality, which conceivably might be 'seen' or grasped by the intellect in some way without reliance on comparison with other situations or on simple observation of its exercise, Hume treats to an entirely and justifiably sceptical barrage. Intelligible powers are figments of the philosophical imagination. Yet it is unfortunate that he is led on to adopt the extreme slogan that the distinction between a power and its exercise is entirely frivolous.

The modification of this slogan with which we are already familiar, Hume's identification of power with the probability or possibility that it will be exercised, and his subjectivist treatment of both as a function of our 'passions', comes later in his account, but is, of course, entirely consistent with his famous and central doctrine that the idea of necessity corresponds to a mere feeling of certainty born of habit. This later, modified, theory about power can be seen as springing from two related sources. Firstly, whatever his doubts about the significance of what philosophers say, Hume accepts that it is out of the question to dismiss all talk of power as empty and meaningless. We really do have an 'idea' corresponding to the word 'power'. In order to explain this idea, Hume saw that recognition must be given to the essential part played by 'experience of the past' in our knowledge of the existence of powers. Secondly, and on the other hand, he is incapable of accepting that this feature of the verification of the statement that x has a power is compatible with the statement's being about x, i.e. with the power's

---

new production is what we infer from the power and the past production.' Hume may here have Locke in mind (cf. *Essay*, Bk II, Ch. XXI, Sect. 1), but even Locke would hardly have approved of *this* argument. Locke does, however, imply that we can see a necessary connection between solidity, *qua* sensible quality, and impenetrability, which is a power; and that all powers are in principle intelligible in this way.

being a real property of x. Now the claim that the powers, the potentialities of a thing are not properties of it, nor a part of its real nature, is a wild paradox, but one for which it is possible to arouse some sympathy, since we can fairly readily be brought to wonder why experience of other things should be essential to knowing a fact about this thing.

Hume's own argument is tied in with an extremely curious, incoherent and pernicious view, the renowned principle of empiricism deriving from Locke, that every idea or concept we have is a copy of a single 'impression' on our sensibility caused by an object, 'external' or 'internal', corresponding to the idea. Since the concepts of power and necessity cannot be derived from a single impression made on us by an object outside us, they cannot refer to such an object. Hume consequently saw his subjectivist view, that these ideas refer to an inner state excited by the series of 'past experiences', as the only way of accounting for them.

An unparadoxical and reasonable theory, however, such as we should all be eager to supply, must explain how, although Hume is quite right to criticise the conception of 'intelligible' powers or necessary connections, and is also right to insist on the importance of comparison with parallel cases, 'experience of the past', yet it is still true that to say that a thing has a certain power *is* to say something about the nature of that thing in particular, and nothing about an observer's feelings, or his past experience, or, for that matter, anything else. We may neglect the unimportant fact that sometimes when we talk of an object's having a power we are evidently saying more about an experiencing subject than we are about the object: e.g., 'A mouse is capable of terrifying her.'

3. EPISTEMOLOGY AND DETERMINISM

There are, traditionally, three plausible but wrong epistemological attitudes towards power, all represented in the argument of Hume's *Treatise*. We may call them *transcendentalism* (or realism), *scepticism* and *reductionism*. They are interrelated, and are also all related to determinism.

a. *Transcendentalism.* There is obviously an epistemological difference between predicates like 'is powerful' or 'can lift ten tons' and predicates like 'is brightly coloured' or 'is round'. We do sometimes talk of seeing and hearing the power of an engine as we talk of seeing its colour or hearing its whine. But its being powerful is not just a matter of how it looks or sounds, as is its being red or its making a noise. Similarly the addition of an ingredient to petrol may involve an increment to its power, but the extra power of the petrol is not the ingredient under another description. It is not another ingredient either. A different kind of difference is involved, which is why there is a philosophical problem at all. One philosophical tendency to obscure this difference, with paradoxical consequences, is the transcendentalist or realist approach to powers, which represents them as 'real' properties, like sensible properties, except that they are beyond our power to perceive.

One way of marking the difference is by saying that the ingredients of the petrol are only contingently connected with its power, and another is to say that we can know of the existence of the ingredients directly, but of the power only indirectly or inductively. The mechanic who instantly 'sees' or 'hears' the power of the engine is relying not only on his sight and hearing, but on his experience of other engines and their performances. But simply to insist on the contingency of the connection and on the necessity of induction is to restrict oneself to the platitudinous and unrevealing. Of course, if we lift the bonnet we shall see an engine but not its power, and of course we have to base our judgement that it is powerful on experience. It is exactly this difference from the judgement that it is red that is frequently marked by the anti-Humean realist when he admits that powers, potentialities and forces are mysterious, occult, unobservable entities. We must realise that by this very admission he tends also to obscure the distinction: for a hidden and unobservable rabbit is no different in itself from a rabbit in full view, as we may readily discover when it is finally produced from the hat. The point that there is no parallel procedure which might enable us to apprehend a potentiality or power 'directly', so that 'indirect' means are the best we can ever hope for, is one which must be seen to hold in principle, and so to reflect the logical nature of powers. It does not just happen that however quickly we lift the bonnet we are never able to see the horsepower. Consequently, the notion that there is something mysterious or occult about powers must not be taken too seriously. To do so is to reify power: that is, to represent it as if it were a property just like redness, only with the lights permanently off.

It is not quite true, of course, that inductive evidence, if this means reference to other things and their performances, or to past performances of the thing in question, is the best we can hope for in order to verify the existence of a power. For we can always in principle, and often in practice conduct a direct test. Indeed, a natural remark to make about the difference between 'This is red' and 'This can do 100 m.p.h.' is that we can see immediately whether this is red but must find out whether it can do 100 m.p.h.; which may suggest that there *is* available to us a procedure of 'finding out' just like the procedure for finding out whether there is a rabbit in the hat. But this natural remark obviously cannot be interpreted in this natural way, since it would then be self-defeating, implying that no real distinction exists to be remarked on. We must respect the difference between finding out that a car in a garage has a certain colour by bringing it into the daylight, and finding out that it can do 100 m.p.h. by taking it for a spin. In the one case we discover that it has the colour by directly observing the colour, in the other we discover that it has the power, not by observing the power but by observing a performance. In a way, the realist will actually stress this difference by misrepresenting the latter discovery as dependent upon an inference from effect to cause, from the observed event to 'a power capable of producing it'.[1] The power thus retains the status of an occult entity, and the realist can still be accused of thinking of it as a quality in principle discoverable by some more direct means, something like a rabbit metaphysically condemned to existence in a hat. But the deductive inference from *p* to *p is possible* is obviously not an inference from effect to cause. In this simple point lies the refutation of realism.

On the other hand, Hume's anti-realism allows for the immediacy of this inference simply by the outright denial of any real distinction between having a power and observably performing. If 'the distinc-

[1] Hume, op. cit., Bk I, Pt III, Sect. XIV. This is Hume's not unjustified interpretation of Locke's remarks on power. He elsewhere deals with Locke's suggestion that we are immediately aware of our own powers (op. cit., *Appendix*).

tion betwixt power and its exercise is entirely frivolous', then when we see the performance we really do see the power. The objection to this, of course, is that *p is possible* does not entail *p*. We can find out, by direct observation, that a car is not red in the same way as we find out that it is red. Whereas even if observing that a car is doing 100 m.p.h. is finding out 'directly' that it can, simply observing that it is not doing 100 m.p.h. does not constitute finding out that it cannot. The fact that powers cannot conceivably be directly observed to be absent is a crucial aspect of what leads to the notion of their transcendental existence, an aspect that Hume fails signally to explain.

b. *Scepticism.* If it is asserted of a car standing in a garage that it can do 100 m.p.h., the assertion may be supported in a number of ways, which we may group, very roughly, as follows:

1. By reference to the fact that it has done 100 m.p.h.
2. By reference to the fact that it is a Jaguar, and Jaguars have done 100 m.p.h., or that it is like other cars, X, Y, and Z, which have done 100 m.p.h.

These we might describe as appeals to 'past experience'. We might also support the assertion by carrying out fresh observations and tests, i.e.,

3. We might simply wait until someone takes out the car, and observe whether it does 100 m.p.h.
4. We might positively test it, trying to make it do 100 m.p.h.
5. We might observe or test similar cars.

This account is simplified in at least one dimension, of course, since tests and observations do not have to be of cars in order to be relevant. But it will do.

In his discussion of necessity and power, Hume never clearly distinguishes between past experience, the conjunction of two kinds of event in the past which, he says, produces the customary transition of the mind from one to the other, which in turn gives rise to our idea of necessity, from the constant conjunction throughout all time, future as well as past, which is implied in the notion of causation and 'constitutes the very essence of power or connection' (p. 163). The omission is not surprising, since to repair it might seem to require a distinction awkward for his form of empiricism, between the content of an idea and the experience that gives rise to it. Of course, trivially, any observation or test, in order to provide support for an assertion, must have occurred, i.e. be past. Yet a reference to 'past experience' cannot explain the content of the notions of causality and power, since it does not allow for the relevance of experience after the time to which the judgement refers, or at least of experience after the time at which the judgement is made.

Admittedly, in the first of his two definitions of a cause, 'an object precedent and contiguous to another, and where all the objects resembling the former are placed in like relations of precedency and contiguity to those objects, that resemble the latter', the grammatically present-tensed verb 'is placed' can be interpreted as logically tenseless, to encompass the future as well as the past. Such an interpretation is supported by his 'rules by which to judge of causes and effects', in which Hume explicitly discusses the importance of conducting experiments before forming a judgement about causal connections, rather than relying on past observations alone. Yet even if we accept the doubtful postulate that Hume understood his first definition to say something about the content as well as the origin of particular causal judgements, it cannot be denied that he seems unaware of the real significance of the shift from past to present tense, and of his remarks about experiment. In the *Enquiry*, as an example of the application of his apparently tenseless definition, he gives the proposition 'that this vibration is followed by this sound, and that all similar vibrations *have been* followed by similar sounds' (my italics).

It is, then, important to allow specifically for the relevance of future observations to the verification of an ascription of unexercised power. I shall argue that it is also important to refer specifically to tests and experiments, as opposed to passive observations. The list given above, however, does seem to cover the possible ways of justifying such an assertion, apart from an appeal to authority. If none of the items listed can provide rational support for it, nothing can. That none of them can is the position of the sceptic.

Scepticism is an approach of fundamental importance in philosophy not so much because it is a theory that many philosophers are eager to embrace, as because it is one that they struggle to avoid. Sceptical arguments tend to provide the background noise of epistemology. But they also play a more positive part and can appear (although often strangely transformed) in the argumentation of philosophers of an at any rate superficially different colour. The sceptic is not really so far from the transcendentalist who represents powers as mysterious properties, or as properties the presence of which can only be known in a mysterious way, intuited perhaps, or 'understood', or which must be 'supposed'. On the other hand, an empiricist like Hume can also adopt, in his discussion of power, the authentic tones of the sceptic.

How sound or 'conclusive' are our proposed methods of justification? The second and the fifth will soon be dismissed by any self-respecting sceptic as hopelessly indirect and untrustworthy. How can observations of other cars be good evidence for a claim about this car? But the first, third and fourth may fare no better, since it will be said that what a car has achieved in the past is no proof that it can do the same now, while what happens after it has left the garage is no proof of its capacities while it was inside. These arguments are abetted by what is correct and undeniable, namely the fact that we can readily think of situations in which a confidence based on true grounds that fall under one or other of our heads may nevertheless be quite unreasonable. It might very well be unreasonable to conclude that one's own car can do what other members of the same class achieve at Monte Carlo, or to assume that it can still do what it used to do, or even to suppose that it has always been able to do what it is doing now.

Our list leaves room for a range of sceptical positions. For example, past performance might be admitted as good grounds, but nothing else; or only future performance; or both past and future performance, but not the performance of other cars. On the last view, if a car never does 100 m.p.h. during its whole life, it cannot be known that it could have done it. But even if all the methods of justification we have mentioned are rejected, we have still not yet arrived at extreme scepticism about power, which shows itself in some arguments of Hume and others, and which is the view that even when a car is actually doing 100 m.p.h. now, we cannot know that it possesses a power. For at best we can only guess or suppose that what we observe is the effect of such a power. Perhaps the power is not there. This argument involves only one step more than is taken by the realist who represents the inference from performance to power, from *p* to *p is possible*, as an inference from effect to cause.

One form of scepticism consists in a denial of existence rather than a denial of knowledge. For those who accept that knowledge of something is impossible can reasonably move to the conclusion that the thing itself does not exist. It is a valid argument that if there is no good reason for supposing the existence of something, then we should not believe in it, any more than in the existence of Gorgons and Harpies.

c. *Reductionism*. One kind of response to such doubts and denials is a reductionism like Hume's. For Hume's position can be seen as a possible answer to scepticism, since by identifying power with its exercise he offers an interpretation of the concept of power that leaves no footholds for scepticism. If the realist is guilty of making a 'frivolous' and unintelligible distinction between power and its exercise, then so is the sceptic who tries to drive a wedge between our knowledge of an action and our knowledge of the power to perform it. Yet although Hume's theory can be opposed to scepticism in this way, it is actually supported by quasi-sceptical arguments. For his route to the conclusion that power is nothing beyond the action is by the argument that nothing can be known of the power beyond what can be known of the action, and that consequently our idea of a power, as something outside us, cannot go beyond our idea of its exercise. There is a strong logical link between scepticism and transcendentalism, but in general an even stronger bond of sympathy between scepticism and reductionism.

There is a variety of degrees of reductionism corresponding to the possible degrees of scepticism. Hume himself manifests two of them: the first of which reduces power to only the very best evidence for its existence, i.e. its present exercise, while the second, the reduction of power to the probability of its exercise, allows for the relevance of 'experience of the past'. We shall soon consider a third, more recent and more sophisticated variety, which attempts to cover all the relevant kinds of justification by introducing, more clearly than Hume, the notion of a tenseless conjunction.

If we can sometimes trace a love-hate relationship between realism and scepticism or between scepticism and reductionism, these epistemological doctrines are nevertheless sufficiently different for it to be at least mildly surprising that they should all be so liable to end up at the same queer conclusion about the *range* of power and possibility: that only what happens can happen, or could have happened. Perhaps this is at first sight most surprising in the case of realism, for it might be expected that the more 'reality' accorded to the power behind the act, the higher the ontological status granted to unexercised powers and unactualised possibilities. One reason why this is generally not so is, of course, that the realist is often eager to argue that everything happens because of a 'real' necessity or connection between events, which serves to make all actual sequences intelligible. Now if everything happens necessarily there is no room for unexercised power, and so the invisible world of real powers is supposed simply to reduplicate the actual course of events, possessing an existence that is shadowy in more ways than one. Moreover, the conception of a power as a 'real' quality or thing behind and producing every act or event has itself tended to link the notion of power closely with the idea that events happen inevitably, rather than with a respect for unactualised possibilities. Powers are thought of as what positively bring events about. This is perhaps one reason why Hume can sometimes treat the notion of power as if it were identical with that of necessity, although it may not entirely explain why he should allege that 'power', 'force', 'necessity', 'connection' are 'all nearly synonymous'. There is a certain naturalness about the talk, in contemporary physics, of 'powers' or forces always in operation, as gravity is continuously in operation, not merely when some body falls.

Scepticism and reductionism are direct routes to determinism. The sceptic who goes so far as to argue that power does not exist unless it is exercised is, of course, already a determinist, since he is an actualist. An extreme reductionism, like that of Hume, is in the same boat, differing from scepticism only by the gloss that no coherent *meaning* can be given to the assertion that something possesses a power, beyond the assertion that it exercises it.[1]

Before we dub Hume a determinist, however, we should remember that he is concerned to argue not only that the idea of power does not refer to anything real 'in' the object, but also that necessity is nothing

---

[1] For the route by which Hume's less extreme position leads to determinism, *v.* Ch. 2, Section 1 above.

real 'in' sequences of events. He is therefore strongly inclined to deny the corollary of actualism, which we have called necessitarianism. This point cannot, of course, be brought in his defence. On the contrary, it constitutes a rather obvious self-contradiction in his theory, which is one of the reasons why it can seem impossible to know just what Hume means on the subject of determinism. For if nothing really has the power of doing what it does not actually do, then everything does what it does necessarily. While if nothing really does what it does necessarily, then everything is capable of doing something other than what it actually does. This contradiction follows from, and, of course, refutes, Hume's brand of empiricism, applied as it is with admirable consistency to correlative concepts.

Direct theorising about the scope of our knowledge of power and necessity, or about explanation, knowledge, understanding and inference in general, is not the only road to determinism. Yet it is worth recognising what an important part overtly epistemological theories do play. Few authors have had a more enduring effect on the freewill controversy than Hume, and his main views on the subject flow directly from the most characteristic and central features of his epistemology.

4. AN ANALYSIS PROPOSED AND DEFENDED

This somewhat general discussion of epistemology and its pitfalls supplies only the prolegomena to an explanation of potentiality. Briefly, the position here taken up is as follows. The procedure for settling the question, e.g. whether a particular car can do 100 m.p.h., should not be taken to imply that powers are properties in any way occult or hidden, even if, truistically, they are not sensible properties. We should also avoid the paradoxical conclusion that they are not really properties. The difficulty arises because reference to other cars and their performances and, in general, to situations other than the situation in question, is not merely an 'indirect' method of conducting the inquiry, in the way in which reference to other cars and their colours would be an indirect way of settling the question whether a certain car was red. That reference to parallel cases is essentially relevant comes out most clearly when we think of the proposition that a power is absent. Nevertheless, such propositions are about the properties of the particular car at a particular time. They are not about other cars, nor are they merely the expression of our feelings.

Let us now consider a suggestion which springs from an objection to the reduction of power to its exercise, whether present, past or future, actual or probable. The objection is that a thing may rightly be said to possess a power that has never and will never be exercised – and that is even certain not to be – provided that in *some* circumstances it *would* be exercised. It may correspondingly be suggested that *x can do a* means (or may be 'analysed into') *In some circumstances, x would do a*; and that, in general, *It is possible for x to be k* means *In some circumstances, x would be k*. This analysis will, of course, supply an analysis of necessity: *x is necessarily k = It is not the case that in some circumstances x would not be k*, i.e. *In no circumstances would x be not-k* or *x would be k in all (or any) circumstances*.

Accordingly the claim that this knife could inflict a nasty wound would be equivalent to the claim that in some circumstances it would do so. And the assertion that this seedling necessarily grows towards the light is to be interpreted as the assertion that it would grow towards the light in any circumstances, i.e. however the conditions might be varied.

As this explanation will be used to uncover more facts about power, it will be necessary to consider a number of possible objections to it.

First, it may be argued that our analysis will inevitably be useless. For if there is some difficulty over the nature of potentiality and the verification of possibility-statements, the same sort of difficulty also arises with regard to hypothetical statements: for example, we need to explain why reference to other occasions than the occasion in question is a primary feature of the verification of hypotheticals.

Now it is certainly true that problems do attach to hypotheticals, yet our analysis can hardly be said to be thereby incapable of contributing at all to our comprehension of potentiality, since, as we have seen, it actually constitutes an objection to Hume's misidentification of power with its exercise. We may also use it to counteract his notion that attributions of power are merely reflections of our past experience. In order to find out whether something would happen in *some* circumstances it is clearly appropriate to set about varying the circumstances, as well as to recall past experience. It might be retorted that it should be just as immediately obvious that in order to find out whether something is possible it is appropriate to conduct tests and experiments. But this is not necessarily as obvious, as we can understand if we reflect on the openings which exist for the Humean confusion between potentiality and epistemic possibility, *possible for* and *possible that*. The hypothetical should free us from this confusion at least. Moreover, the analysis might also help to reduce the inclination to think of powers as occult quasi-sensible properties or entities.[1] As we might put it, the hypothetical carries on its face, more clearly than does the ascription of potentiality, its method of verification or logical type. It must of course be granted that we have not achieved a transformation or translation of ascriptions of power into statements that have none of their verificational peculiarities or difficulties. I should contend that this ideal of much 'analytic' philosophy is impossible, but in any case my answer to this line of criticism must simply be a request to wait and see what further clarification can be achieved by the move I have made.

There is a further question that should be broached, which arises from the criticism not that an analysis into hypotheticals is merely useless, but that it is a positively false step, away from understanding and light. This is because it is supposed to raise the peculiarly murky problem of 'counterfactual', 'unfulfilled' or 'subjunctive' conditionals. One writer, for example, remarks that:

> It ought to be, but plainly is not, generally known to philosophers that the logic of counterfactual conditionals is a very ill-explored territory; no adequate formal logic for them has yet been devised . . . It is really a scandal that people should count it a philosophical advance to adopt a programme of analysing ostensible categoricals into unfulfilled conditionals.[2]

[1] But cf. Bradley: *Logic*, Bk I, Ch. II. Bradley argues that we can only make sense of hypothetical statements if we understand them to be predicating dispositions of reality – a curious reversal of current treatment of dispositional statements, but a nice instance of the power of realism. Note that Bradley's dispositions, the ground of hypothetical judgements, are 'latent or occult' qualities.

[2] P. T. Geach: *Mental Acts*, p. 6. cf. also A. I. Melden: *Free Action*, p. 110, and S. Hampshire: 'Subjunctive Conditionals', *Analysis*, 1948, p. 13.

Since, as it happens, we could hardly have continued in our investigation into the nature of power without drawing attention to the connection with hypotheticals, without discussing the relation between *if* and *cans*, we need to pause in order to remove this sort of obstacle from our path.

First, it is simply a misconception that there is a special problem about the class of 'unfulfilled' or 'counterfactual' empirical conditionals, if this description is meant to refer to conditional statements of which the protasis or antecedent supposition is in fact false. It is a mistake to suppose that there *could* be a problem about the 'logic', or verification, of such a class. It is the same kind of mistake as would be made by someone who thought that a special logic is required for false statements as opposed to true ones. This can be made quite obvious by a single example. The utterance, 'If Smith is there, Jones is there too. But if Smith is not there, Jones is not there either', contains two conditionals. Supposing that they have the same reference, one of them, necessarily, will be fulfilled, the other unfulfilled, although we may not know which. Yet they are both, clearly, of the same logical type, and the difference between them is logically and philosophically trivial.

The expression 'counterfactual conditional', however, is often misleadingly used interchangeably with 'subjunctive conditional' to refer, not to conditionals which are as a matter of fact unfulfilled, but to conditionals which are cast in the subjunctive mood or in what, in English, passes for the subjunctive. The latter class is quite unlike the former. Mood is at least the kind of thing that might affect the sense of a statement, and in fact it normally does. The question is whether it affects the sense in such a way as to present a special logical or philosophical problem. The usual view is that it does, since it entails, or seems to entail, that the antecedent is unfulfilled and hence that the statement is in principle undecidable.

The argument depends on two theses or, as they often are, presuppositions. The first is that, if a conditional statement is unfulfilled, it is unverifiable or undecidable; i.e. that it can only be known whether 'If p, then q' is true or false if p is true. This view, as it stands, does not involve the crude mistake of supposing that unfulfilled conditionals comprise a special kind of statements with peculiar logical characteristics, since it is a thesis about all conditionals, that there is no way of verifying them unless they are fulfilled.

The second thesis is that the subjunctive mood of 'If *p were* the case, *q would be* the case' affects the sense of the conditional so that it entails that *p* is not the case, and so (in view of the first supposition) is like adding 'and this is unverifiable' to the conditional. Consequently we can never know the statement to be true, since it will either be unverifiable or false. This is contrary to our intuitions, which is presumably why it is supposed to create a problem for logic.

The second thesis is obviously less important than the first, and in fact has no remarkable consequences except in combination with the first. Nevertheless it is worth noticing that it is mistaken. If it were true, then whenever someone says something like 'If it were to rain, the fire would go out' and it then proceeds to rain, his assertion would automatically be false. Yet it seems clear that if the rain goes on to put out the fire, his assertion would normally be regarded as having been shewn to be true. The same applies to conditionals about the past. It is true that no one would say, except disingenuously or inappropriately, 'If it had rained, the fire would have gone out', unless he believes that it did not rain. Someone who makes this assertion probably also believes that the fire did not go out. But if both these beliefs are mistaken, his hypothetical assertion, so far from being certainly false, is very likely true.

A subjunctive hypothetical carries an implication that its antecedent is unfulfilled (or, as the *O.E.D.* puts it, that it is a 'mere hypothesis') in something like the way in which the question 'Didn't it rain?' carries an implication that it rained. Is 'Didn't it rain?' the same question as 'Did it rain?', or as 'Did it *rain*?', or as '*Did* it rain?' It is, in as much as all necessarily have the same right answer. In this way 'If the bough broke, the cradle fell' and 'If the bough had broken, then the cradle would have fallen' may both be forms of the same statement, such that necessarily they both have the same truth-value. There is thus no peculiar philosophical problem about the truth-value or method of verification of subjunctive conditionals, since it is the same as that of the corresponding indicative conditional; just as there is no special difficulty over how to set about answering questions expecting the answer 'no'. The force of the subjunctive is not to assert that the antecedent is unfulfilled, although the mood does in effect *hint* that this is so.

It is worth turning to the first and more interesting thesis on which the notion of a special class of hypotheticals of peculiar logical or epistemological opacity is based, the thesis that an ordinary empirical conditional statement is unverifiable if it is not fulfilled. Such a view corresponds to the sceptical position that we cannot know that a car is *capable* of doing 100 m.p.h. unless the capacity is exercised. It is also obviously related to scepticism about the future, since I now know that I should die if I drank a tumbler full of cyanide, with the same certainty as, if I drank a tumbler full of cyanide, I could then expect to die. This sort of example might mislead us into absolutely identifying scepticism about unfulfilled conditionals with scepticism about the future. But dissatisfaction with the verifiability of hypotheticals, like the difficulties over the status of powers, springs from more than the straightforward 'Problem of Induction'. This much is intimated in our attempts to *characterise* hypotheticals and ascriptions of power by means of the formula 'Reference to parallels, to "experience of the past", to observations and tests on other occasions, can constitute a satisfactory justification or refutation.' Any empirical statement – indeed, any statement whatsoever – is capable of being justified or refuted on the basis of inductive evidence. We must therefore make it clear that here inductive evidence is peculiarly relevant.

One way of marking the peculiarity would be to say that reference to parallels is not merely indirectly relevant in the way in which the outraged husband's observations that someone else's hat is in the hall and that someone else's boots are under the bed, together with his knowledge of what has been the case on like occasions, are indirectly relevant to his immediate conclusion that there is a man in the wardrobe. The husband's observations are *indirectly* relevant because, although they are highly relevant, one further observation could be made which would settle the matter, whatever such indirect evidence might be: namely, the observation of the man in the wardrobe. On the other hand, we cannot under any circumstances dispense with a knowledge of parallels in order to know to be true 'If Smith drinks the cyanide, he will die.' As it is often pointed out, it is not enough to see Smith drink and die. For we can imagine this happening in a situation in which everyone drinks cyanide all the time without harmful effects and, moreover, in which Smith was evidently just about to die anyway. We should then dismiss the 'direct' evidence for the antecedently asserted hypothetical as coincidental. It is rightly held that there must be a 'connection' between protasis and apodosis. The hypothetical is in this respect more like 'He will die because he will drink it' than it is like 'He will drink it, and then he will die.' 'Indirect' considerations are therefore indispensable, but a ground that is indispensable is hardly indirect.

We have argued that the conception of a power as a hidden property or entity offers a misleading model, because it suggests that the reason why, in answering questions about powers, we cannot dispense with reference to parallels, 'past experience' and so on, is no more than the reason why we cannot dispense with memory and inference, if we are to justify a description of something temporarily hidden from us, for example the colour scheme of a darkened room, or the layout of the garden over a wall. In the same way, the model of the occult referent, whether a mysterious 'connection', a latent 'disposition' or a merely hypothetical state of affairs, represents a disastrous approach to conditional statements. Hypothetical events are not events hidden from us in another world, so that we can only infer their nature. This is precisely because it is false that 'the occurrence of events which falsify the antecedent of a subjunctive conditional makes it impossible to determine the truth-value of the conditional in much the same way as a high wall makes it impossible to see what is on the other side', to quote from a recent attempt to dissolve the problem about the verifiability of hypotheticals by reducing it to the 'Problem of Induction'.[1] On the contrary, if there is a general problem about empirical conditionals, it finds expression in the question, 'How is it that what is true of other things in other situations is *more* than indirectly relevant to the determination of a question about this thing, or this situation?' In the next section, we shall see that the same question, *mutatis mutandis*, can be asked about universal conditionals; although there are some empirical hypotheticals, or quasi-hypotheticals, of which it would be pointless to ask it, e.g. 'If he is speaking, I do not hear him.' But if this

[1] J. Watling: 'The Problem of Contrary-to-Fact Conditionals', *Analysis*, 1956-7.

is ever a problem, it is evidently not a problem specific to hypotheticals, let alone 'counterfactual' or 'subjunctive' hypotheticals, since it is exactly the question that we have independently been led to ask about powers.

We may notice a difference: whereas a single observation may conclusively verify that something possesses a power (p entails that p is possible), more than a single observation is required to verify a conditional like our examples ('p and q' does not entail 'if p, then q'). On the other hand, a single observation can conclusively falsify the latter but not the former (p and not q' entails that 'If p, then q' is false. 'Not p' does not entail that p is not possible). This difference can be explained, on the present analysis, as a corollary of the difference between a hypothetical in which the antecedent is left unspecific, 'In some circumstances, q', and one with a specific antecedent, 'If p, then q.' It also corresponds to the difference between the powers and capacities of things on the one hand, and their dispositional or causal properties on the other. The latter are, of course, very commonly explained by means of 'specific' hypotheticals. If a thing breaks, we know that it *can* break, but we need to know more about the causes of its breaking, whether it was struck by a teaspoon or a steam-hammer, before we can conclude that it is fragile or brittle.

This obvious distinction will prove profoundly important in another area, when we come to consider the powers of people. It is perhaps in elucidating such distinctions, rather than in making any great contribution towards the solution of more general epistemological difficulties about 'unobservable' properties, that the present analysis of natural power has its chief utility.

5. POWER AND LAW

The argument that this analysis achieves little would perhaps be more serious if a positive alternative were offered that clearly achieves much more. I shall therefore devote a short space to criticism of a popular rival theory. This is the view that ascriptions of power and, for that matter, all hypothetical statements are really universal or general statements, or incorporate them. It is very commonly stated that 'p is empirically possible' always means the same as 'It is not a law that $\sim p$.'

As it stands, this suggestion cannot be taken very seriously, since 'It is not a law that my car does not do 100' is simply nonsense just because there cannot be laws of nature about particular cars. It is equally clear that we cannot save the theory simply by generalising 'my car' as 'cars', since it does not follow from the general fact that it is possible that a car (*some* car) should do 100 m.p.h. that *this* car can. The view is sometimes taken that some more specific description is 'understood', and that this must supply the first term in the law-statement. This would make the sentence 'This car can do 100 m.p.h.' indefinitely ambiguous, and is another instance in which an inclination to dub a whole class of statements 'elliptical' is a fair indication that it has been misunderstood.

A more promising suggestion is the view that while no specific law-statement is actually enunciated, or requires to be understood, a law-statement is, so to speak, obliquely mentioned without being specified. According to this account, 'This car can do 100 m.p.h.' means something like 'It is (in general) possible that anything like this car should do 100 m.p.h.', which may in turn be explained as 'It is not a law that things like this car do not do 100 m.p.h.'; and thus every particular power is supposed to consist in a general possibility, which is the negation of a law, although which possibility and which law is determined only by the indefinite expression 'like this'. Another way of putting it would be, 'Let (some of) the properties of this car be ϕ, then it is not a law that anything ϕ does not do 100 m.p.h.'

What does this kind of suggestion achieve? There are various motives for seeing the particular as logically subordinate to the general, few if any of them reputable, but a special reason for preferring general possibilities to particular powers is evidently that if the assertion about the power of this car can be seen as really being an assertion about all cars like this, we might seem to have a simple explanation for just what was puzzling, namely the relevance of evidence about the performance of these other cars, an explanation which takes us out of the charmed circle of statements with the awkward characteristic of an irremediably indirect-seeming verification, and which would therefore appear much superior to my own analysis. This account might also seem to offer a simple and straightforward explanation of how something can possess a power that is never exercised: being essentially general, the existence and real exercise of the power consists as much in the performance of things like its 'possessor', as in that of the 'possessor' itself.

Apart from other considerations which will appear later, the attractiveness of the theory is greatly diminished if it is realised that just the same issues arise at the level of generality as may perplex us at the level of the particular, and that consequently the move to the general cannot be supposed to have settled them. There is the traditional distinction between 'universals of fact' and 'universals of law' (*v.*, e.g., W. E. Johnson: *Logic*, Part III, Ch. I): the assertion that every actual raven has been, is and will be black, or that there never has been and never will be a raven that is not black, does not constitute an assertion that it is a law that ravens are black, or that a non-black raven is *impossible*. This point precisely parallels the objection to the view that a power consists in its exercise, past, present or future. A power may exist unexercised by its possessor, but a general possibility may equally well fail ever to be actualised. To deny this is simply to accept the Humean paradox, but at the level of generality, that there is no distinction between a possibility and its actualisation, that *p is possible* entails *p*. An explanation that includes this kind of paradox is, to say the least, no explanation. As Johnson puts it, 'the affirmation of law, or nomic necessity, implies the factual universal; but the negation of law – i.e. the affirmation of nomic contingency – does not imply the factual particular'.

The distinction between 'fact' and 'law' is easier to draw than to explain, which may be one reason why it is so often challenged. But it is evident that universal necessity-statements and possibility-statements possess verificational features like those that we have attributed to particular statements. Most importantly, reference to situations that are not *instances* of the *class* in question play an essential part in their verification. From experience of things other than cobalt bombs, fortunately, we can conclude that a cobalt bomb explosion is possible. That is why even general possibilities need not be actualised.

We can congratulate ourselves on the fact that our own analysis helps to explain general as well as particular possibilities and necessities.

A cobalt bomb explosion is possible if in some circumstances such an explosion would take place. Ravens are necessarily black if no variation in conditions would produce a raven that is not black. Our analysis simply reflects what has often been noted, that a law-statement cannot be satisfactorily supported by a simple aggregation of instances, but must be tested in a variety of conditions: as it is sometimes put, it is important to try hard to produce a counter-instance. On the other hand, it is not in the same way appropriate to talk of *testing* a prediction, even an 'open' or general prediction, i.e. a 'universal of fact'. This is related to the point that it is always in principle possible to make a prediction true or false, although never, of course, logically possible to do anything to affect the truth-value of a law-statement. Someone says that there will be no cobalt explosions, and we can build the bomb to make his statement false. Alternatively we can take measures to prevent his claim from being made false. But the assertion that a cobalt explosion is impossible is not the kind of claim that can be made true or false. Its truth or falsity can simply be discovered. It can simply be tested.

J. S. Mill's definition of the cause of a phenomenon as 'the antecedent, or the concurrence of antecedents, on which the phenomenon is invariably and *unconditionally* consequent' implies, of course, an analysis like our own. As Mill puts it, 'that which is necessary, that which *must* be, means that which will be, whatever supposition we may make in regard to all other things'. But it is doubtful whether he saw that his explanation should raise more problems than it settles for a supporter of Hume. The same criticism may be made of P. F. Strawson's more recent use of a Millian analysis as a way of explaining an aspect of the confirmation of law-statements. Strawson rejects the naïve view that the degree to which a law-statement has been confirmed is simply a function of the number of positive instances of the purported law that have been observed. The range or variety of the instances must also be considered. Common sense is supported by the strict paradox that would otherwise result. Suppose that all ACs are As but not all As are ACs, and that we have observed a very large number of ACs which are B, but have not observed, in the case of any other, perhaps very different kind of A, whether it is B. 'All As are B' and 'All ACs are B' are thereby supported by an equal number of instances.

Yet they obviously cannot be supposed to be equally confirmed. This may be attributed to the fact that the range of these instances is necessarily less in relation to the wider, than in relation to the narrower generalisation.[1]

But Strawson's own account is inadequate. He states that a generalisation is confirmed '(1) in proportion as our observations of instances of As which are Bs is numerous, and (2) in proportion as the variety of conditions in which the instances are found is wide'. But these too strict requirements leave unexplained, for example, how a law with *no* actual instances can be confirmed by deduction from, and therefore to the same degree as, another well-confirmed law; i.e. how a generalisation can be confirmed by observations which are not observations of its instances at all. By the same token, his account fails to give due weight to the importance of such parallel cases in confirming any law-statement, however frequently seen to be instantiated; just as a failure to recognise the peculiar, more than 'indirect' relevance of parallels in supporting an unfulfilled conditional goes with a failure to recognise their indispensability even when the protasis and apodosis are both seen to be fulfilled.

---

[1] *An Introduction to Logical Theory*, pp. 245-7. By an ingenious but fallacious argument (in which he confuses counting classes or properties with counting particular instances) Strawson, having recognised the requirement of range, tries to reduce it to a matter of the number of instances. It is actually with particular reference to this argument that he uses the formulation 'In all circumstances, all As are B', but this is unimportant. Cf. Mill: *System of Logic*, Bk III, Ch. V.

5
Some Puzzles about Potentiality

1. INTRODUCTORY

In the next two sections of this chapter I shall consider some further objections to the hypothetical analysis of natural possibility, that is, to the equation of *x can do a* with *Under some circumstances, x will do a*. The purpose of the discussion is not simply to achieve precision, for it is not clear that the objections can be dealt with in any very precise way. But they raise issues of fundamental importance to an understanding of possibility and the shortcomings of determinism. Some of their implications will be drawn out in the remainder of the chapter, which constitutes a refutation of actualism, as it applies to natural possibility.

2. THE IDEA OF A 'CIRCUMSTANCE'

If the analysis of possibility presented in the last chapter is to be retained then the notion of a 'circumstance' at least requires some elucidation. For as it stands, the analysis may be taken to imply, absurdly, that provided that we know that any hypothetical is true of which the apodosis is '*x* will do *a*', then we may conclude that *x* can do *a*. But it is clear that, for example, 'This magnet will pick up a nail, if John says that it will' does not imply that the magnet in question can pick up a nail. For the antecedent might be unfulfilled just because John knows that the magnet cannot pick up a nail.

It seems intuitively that this particular kind of counter-example is not damaging, although an exhaustive disquisition on conditionality might be required in order to explain exactly why. Perhaps we can take a short cut by distinguishing two ways of understanding an empirical conditional: firstly as a 'causal' or 'consequential' conditional, implying that the grammatical consequent gives what would be a real consequence of the condition given in the antecedent; and secondly as an 'inferential' conditional, which simply implies that the consequent would be a sound inference from the antecedent. All conditionals understood or meant 'consequentially' are *ipso facto* understood or meant 'inferentially', but not *vice versa*. For example, an editorial pronouncement that, if the reserves are called up, there will be war, might be meant merely inferentially: the editor is giving his readers a tip about the circumstances in which to anticipate war, hide their gold, invest in armaments and so on. On the other hand, the same sentence might be meant not only inferentially but consequentially: the editor is warning us of the conditions that would bring on war, perhaps with a view to discouraging a policy. Now 'This magnet will pick up a nail, if John says that it will' will normally not be meant consequentially, since we do not believe in magic. Hence it will not be meant to imply that this magnet *can* pick up a nail.

Allowance might be made for this point by a modification of the analysans into something like 'Some circumstances would bring it about that x will do a'; but if 'consequential' and 'inferential' conditionals are admitted as different types or categories of empirical conditional, then it need only be said that 'In certain circumstances, x would do a' is consequential.

Another, more revealing, line of objection to the analysis will lead us to try to clarify further the idea of 'circumstance' that is required. 'If this car had been a Rolls Royce, it would have done 100 m.p.h.' and 'If that bar is iron, it will support your weight' might both be normally and reasonably understood as consequential conditionals, but it would be absurd to advance them in support of, respectively, the claim that this car could have done 100 m.p.h. and the claim that that bar can support your weight. The analysis must be qualified in order to exclude this kind of case.

If only certain kinds of example are considered, the suggestion might seem reasonable that the conditions or circumstances hypothesised should be 'efficient' rather than 'underlying' causes, events rather than states. Such an explanation might seem to distinguish

A. *If this car had eight cylinders, it would do* 100 *m.p.h.* from
B. *If this car were driven properly, it would do* 100 *m.p.h.* and
C. *If this were a match, it would make a light* from
D. *If this were struck, it would make a light.*
Of each pair of statements, the first would not support the attribution of a potentiality, while the second would.

Other examples prove that this cannot be the correct explanation. If we compare
E. *If the starter were replaced, the car would start easily* with
F. *If the choke is out, the car will start easily*, and with
G. *If the tank is full, etc.*,
we can see that the difference between 'efficient' and 'underlying' causes is unimportant. The replacement of a starter is an event, but it is E that would not imply that the car *can* start easily.

The correct principle by which to range such examples as A, C and E against B, D, F and G is that the subordinate clauses of the former all relate to something in some sense 'internal' or intrinsic to the subject, affecting its nature or 'essence'. The differences envisaged in B, D, F and G, however, are extrinsic or inessential. The theory under consideration must, of course, be interpreted as the suggestion that '*x* could do *a*' means that in certain *extrinsic* conditions, in some *external* circumstances, *x* would do *a*.

It should be made clear that 'essence' here does not mean 'definition', or anything like it. Particular things do not have essences in that sense. Nevertheless, the distinction between the intrinsic and the extrinsic, the essential and the inessential properties of a thing is liable to meet with objections. But its introduction is necessary for an explanation of potentiality. If there are difficulties in the distinction it is nevertheless one that is presupposed in much speech and thought, including the commonest notion of a 'condition' or 'circumstance'. It would be a lie or a joke to blame the 'conditions' for the failure of a crop when we know that the cause of the failure was inferior seed. If someone alleged that his car would have won the race in better conditions, we should count it a poor argument that it would have won if it had been a better car. Such everyday distinctions may not exactly correspond to the one we want between extrinsic and intrinsic conditions. For whatever reason, we do not normally regard the skill of a driver or the pressure he puts on the accelerator as one of the 'conditions' in which his car is performing. A match that is advertised to light 'in all conditions' will be required to put up a satisfactory performance when struck in wind and rain; but we should hardly expect it to burst into flames in the smoker's pocket. We need only take the point that a perfectly ordinary and intelligible notion of the 'conditions' affecting something is of conditions at least extrinsic to the nature of that thing.

It is relevant to reflect on what it is to test something. Giving a car a test may involve filling the tank and driving it out of the garage, but if we proceed to change its engine, we are doing more than just testing it. Indeed, a major alteration in the car would preclude us from testing its original capacities. To test x's capacity to do a is not simply to try to bring it about that x does a, but to do so without bringing about a prior change in the nature of x. Of course, a test can result in an essential or intrinsic change in the object, which is why a positive test of the power to explode is characteristically unrepeatable. From 'If the fuse were lit, the gunpowder would explode' we can conclude that the gunpowder is capable of exploding, even though the condition mentioned would involve, in some sense, an intrinsic change in the gunpowder. But in this case the change is itself the actualisation of the potentiality, and not a condition in which the potentiality is actualised. The test-condition is, in itself, an 'extrinsic' matter.

We may notice that the distinction between intrinsic and extrinsic conditions is fundamental to the notion of a 'causal' or 'dispositional' property. The predicates 'fragile', 'brittle', 'acid-sensitive', 'soluble' and the like are commonly subjected to philosophical analysis into hypotheticals, and in each case the proposed antecedent ('If struck or strained ...', 'If placed in acid ...', etc.) which gives the test-conditions appropriate to the particular property, necessarily hypothesises a purely extrinsic modification, even if the actualisation or exercise of the disposition, as given in the consequent, sometimes involves such a major intrinsic change as dissolving, or even ceasing to exist.

All this links up with some of the points made earlier. For example, a refusal to accept Hume's doctrine that power is nothing in the agent beyond its exercise can draw some strength from the present argument, according to which unexercised power is a matter of what its possessor would do, *having* the nature it now has, in conditions *not* affecting its nature. The conceptual link between 'nature' and 'potentiality' is at least very strong. I shall suggest that this is something of an understatement.

Another connection can be made with the point that the verification of '*x* has (or lacks) the power to do *a*' essentially involves reference to 'parallel cases'. In what respects parallel? The important affinities will obviously be affinities of *nature* and not of *situation*. If we want to know whether the car in the garage can do 100 m.p.h., it is the performance of other cars like it in having six cylinders, new engines and the like that has primary relevance, not the performance of other vehicles in garages with the brakes on, or other things seven thousand miles from the North Pole.

3. THE DISTINCTION BETWEEN INTRINSIC AND EXTRINSIC PROPERTIES

We may still face awkward questions about the distinction between intrinsic and extrinsic qualities or properties. *Why* should one property of a thing be regarded as 'intrinsic', a part of its nature, while another is 'extrinsic', external to its nature? Why, when a thing ceases to possess some property, should we think of it sometimes as being itself unaltered, but in altered circumstances, sometimes as having itself undergone a change, and sometimes as having undergone an essential change. Our problem is not a problem about identity through change, but a problem about the different kinds of change a thing can undergo while retaining its identity.

Relational properties would seem to be necessarily 'extrinsic', at least with respect to physical things and substances.[1] A relational change may be the stimulus required for the manifestation of a power (the movement of a magnet in relation to some iron filings or the Earth's poles, for example), but hardly in itself a change in the nature of the object. On the other hand, the presumably relational property

---

[1] Remembering that we attribute potentialities of a kind to, e.g., events and places (cities, deserts, etc.).

of being rubbed against a lode-stone may causally change the nature of its possessor, if this happens to be a bit of iron. Knowing this, we should rightly refuse to attribute to an iron bar the same powers as a magnet simply on the ground that, if it had been rubbed against a lodestone it would have attracted the iron filings that it actually failed to attract. Perhaps this case can be dealt with by means of a stratification of potentialities: non-magnetic iron is potentially capable of attracting pins, wood is not. A magnet, on the other hand, actually has the power.[1]

Qualitative changes, at any rate, may nor may not be 'essential'. It may be that a car with four flat tyres or four dirty plugs out of six will not do 100 m.p.h., however good the driver or the driving conditions. But these attributes would normally be regarded as inessential features of the car when it comes to assessing its capacities. To replace an old, worn-out engine with an efficient, new one is to change the nature of the car, but what goes for engines does not, for some reason, go for tyres. We can refute the proud owner's claims for the capacities of his car by referring to the state of its piston rings, but hardly by pointing to a flat tyre or a loose connection, and certainly not by demonstrating that his gear is at present in neutral. Where do we draw the line? Somewhere, it seems, we shall have a case on the borderline between a minor job for the driver or at most the service station, and a full-scale job for the repair shop. To take another example, we might wonder whether to say of a damp match that it is capable of starting a fire. Perhaps the right answer is 'yes and no'.

The existence or possibility of borderline cases cannot in itself cast doubt on the validity of any distinction. What is more significant is that the distinction between intrinsic and extrinsic observable properties is evidently empirical. Why should altering the position of certain pedals be a part of *testing* a car, while altering the position or shape of some other part would come nearer to a *modification*? This much surely depends on the empirical matter of how a car works, and how to drive it. We can at least imagine a car with a small disposable engine, needing to be changed every morning. We should then consider a change of

[1] It is a wrong reaction (a pseudo-explanation) to proliferate senses, or uses, of *can*: as if in one sense of *can* all iron can attract pins, but in another sense of *can*, only magnets can. Cf. Ryle: *Concept of Mind*, p. 128 f, on allegedly different uses of *can swim*.

engine as we now consider a change of oil, a change but not an essential one – not a change in the car.

It seems, therefore, that the question which of the properties of a thing constitute its 'nature', and which are extrinsic, depends on tests just as much as does any question about its potentialities. Yet our explanation of potentiality seems to require that the nature of a thing is something, i.e. a set of observable properties, other than its powers, independent of them and capable of being independently determined. For if we regard our analysis as an attempt to explain propositions about potentialities by specifying their relation to a particular class of hypotheticals, it would seem to be an embarrassment if the identification of this class could not proceed entirely independently of the notion of a potentiality.

To take a slightly different kind of example, the colour of a car or of a magnet, or, say, the material from which the frames of a pair of spectacles are made, would reasonably be regarded as 'extrinsic' or inessential properties of the car or the spectacles: a red car can be essentially the same, and have just the same nature, as a blue car. Surely the reason is that the powers of these things, or at least their important ones, are not related to these particular qualities as they are to certain structural factors, shape and so on. This we discover from tests.

That the determination of the potentialities of an object or substance cannot be supposed to wait on the prior determination of some set of 'essential' observable properties can be seen from the example of the magnet. The difference between a magnet and a non-magnetic piece of iron is not an observable qualitative difference nor a function of such a difference, since in this case there is no observable qualitative difference. What is observable is simply the exercise of the magnet's powers. The difference between them is a difference in power or disposition, which physics explains by a difference in unobservable structure. It seems wrong to represent a thing's 'nature', as we have tended to represent it, as a set of properties merely related to its potentialities and different from them. A thing's powers characteristically constitute its nature, and, indeed, are largely responsible for our thinking of it as a thing, with a nature, at all. Descartes is right to argue that he cannot observe or 'imagine' the nature of his famous piece of wax, even if he wrongly tends to imply that the essential nature of a material thing never includes determinate observable qualities. Clearly the observable structure of a machine is generally an intrinsic property.

A critique of the programme of philosophical 'analysis' is obviously beyond the scope of this book. I shall only suggest that the relationships between such categories as Material Thing, Nature, Essence, Quality, Potentiality, Act, Disposition, State and Structure should be thought of as forming a network rather than a pyramid, so that we should be satisfied with ultimately reflexive explanations in place of the ancient philosophical ideal of analytic definitions of the complex in terms of the simple. It seems out of the question that the notion of a physical object can be subordinated to the notion of a potentiality, or *vice versa*.[1] It is equally wrong to suppose that the notion of the nature of a thing is prior to the notion of a potentiality, and herein lies our present difficulty in explaining the latter. Nevertheless, we can be grateful that, by presenting something of the relationship between these two notions, we can achieve some understanding of the hardly deniable difference in significance, when it comes to assessing the potentialities of a car, between the fact that it would do 100 m.p.h. if it were differently driven, and the fact that it would do 100 m.p.h. if it were differently constructed.

Finally, and briefly, we might consider a more direct accusation of circularity. This arises from the argument that what a thing is capable of doing cannot consist in what it would do in certain circumstances, since it may be true that such and such an event *would* occur under certain conditions, and yet the event be impossible simply because the necessary conditions are impossible. It may at first seem wrong to suppose that a consequential conditional can be true even if the antecedent is impossible, but this is really quite acceptable. Let us imagine that a scientist, presented with the design of a rocket, can calculate that it would get to Mars if and only if, among other things, it was supplied with a liquid fuel twice as powerful as any at present available. Suppose that he also calculates or discovers that such a fuel is a physical or natural impossibility, contrary to the laws of nature. He can deduce from both of these bits of knowledge together that it is impossible that

[1] Cf. P. Wiggins: 'Identity' in *Analytical Philosophy*, ed. E. J. Butler, p. 69, for a similar point about the interdependence of the *identification* of particulars and their *classification*.

the rocket should get to Mars, by an argument of the following form: q, only if p; p is impossible; therefore q is impossible. The premisses of this argument clearly are compatible.

Now in this case we are faced with a difficulty in determining the power of the rocket. We might say that in theory the rocket is capable of reaching Mars, although no possible fuel is powerful enough to propel it. I do not think that this suggestion is entirely absurd. On the other hand it would be quite misleading to say without qualification that the rocket has the power, and it is reasonable to suggest that this would be misleading because it would be false. If such a view is taken, we are left with the problem of how to deal with all cases in which it is true that in certain circumstances x would do a, although false that x could do a. The only modification to our analysis of possibility that would exclude such cases would also seem to introduce a striking element of circularity. For we should need to expand it into 'In certain *possible* circumstances, x would do a', in which the concept we are trying to explain reappears unanalysed. It is true that the possibility in question is a general possibility rather than a particular potentiality, but, as we have seen, there is no reason for regarding this as an absolute advance.

It seems necessary to admit that we have not succeeded in explaining potentiality away in terms of something else. According to the traditional view of analysis and definition as a sort of intellectual anatomy of complex wholes into simple parts, it now behoves us to conclude that the concept of possibility is simple, unanalysable and therefore inexplicable. Fortunately, as we have suggested, there is no good reason for supposing that the traditional view is correct. Philosophical explanation is not conceptual anatomy, and one way of explaining a concept or class of statements is simply to demonstrate what it is like. It can hardly be denied that asserting that a white raven is possible is very close to asserting that a white raven would be produced in suitable conditions, whatever objections can be raised against an absolute identification of the two or against the view that one of these assertions is in simpler, logically more primitive terms than the other.

It is generally and rightly agreed that something can be achieved towards an understanding of 'causal properties' by treating dispositional statements as hypotheticals. Yet the objections to our explanation of potentiality can all be brought against any paraphrase of '*x* is fragile' in the form of a hypothetical. Faced with a genus of statements with verificational similarities, a genus that includes dispositional statements, general and particular natural possibility-statements, law-statements, causal statements and certain kinds of hypothetical statements, we need not expect that all the species of the genus are reducible to one of their own number without differentiae. It is nevertheless important to find ways of demonstrating the more or less subtle relationships that exist within the genus. It is the function of our analysis to contribute to this elucidation.

4. THE REFUTATION OF ACTUALISM

'Actualism', the doctrine that nothing ever has the power to do what it does not actually do, is generally grounded on the principle that, if an action is caused, it follows that the agent cannot do otherwise. The discussion so far can help to shew that this argument is fallacious, at any rate with respect to inanimate 'agents'.

If a car is not doing 100 m.p.h., but on the contrary is sitting motionless in its garage, we can assume that its inaction has a cause, and that some of the 'necessary conditions' for actual motion are absent. But whether or not the car *can* do 100 m.p.h. depends on the character of this absent factor, these 'necessary conditions'. If the reason for the car's immobility is that it is badly damaged, then no doubt it cannot do 100 m.p.h. But if the reason is simply that it is out of fuel, that the engine is switched off or that the key to the garage is lost, then the mere fact that its immobility has a cause obviously does not mean that it lacks the power of movement. The absent 'necessary conditions' must be present in order that the power should be tested or manifested, but not in order to bring it into existence. This much is common sense, but it is explained and supported by the philosophical distinction that I have made between intrinsic factors, such as serious damage, and extrinsic factors, like petrol in the tank. It can now be seen why a necessary condition for the actualisation of a potentiality is not necessarily a necessary condition for the existence of the potentiality. It is my contention that this principle must be recognised to hold for all empirical possibility – including, as we shall see, possibility for choice – if we are to achieve any understanding of it.

In the abstract, actualism can appear in an undeniably attractive light, even if, like Zeno's paradoxes, it presents an argument that it is ultimately difficult to take quite seriously:

> The actual must at least be ontologically possible. But ontological possibility – unlike the purely logical – does not consist in freedom from contradiction, but in the real series of conditions. In the strict sense a thing is 'really possible', only when the whole series is at hand, down to the last member. On the other side, however, it is then not only possible, but also necessary, that is, it can no longer fail to appear. It could fail to appear, so long as at least one condition in the series was lacking. If that also were added, nothing more could prevent the real actuality. But exactly this inevitability is ontological necessity. The consequence is this: all that is ontologically possible is thereby ontologically necessary also. (N. Hartmann: *Ethics*, Vol. III.)

How are we to relate this strange identification of the actual, the possible and the necessary, to the ordinary conception of a potentiality according to which there certainly is a difference between being capable of doing 100 m.p.h. and actually doing it? Is there perhaps some further, ultimate, question whether it is 'really possible' for a car to do 100 m.p.h., beyond the everyday question whether it can do it? It seems more reasonable to suggest that the author of this passage has simply failed to understand the concept of possibility of which he purports to give an account. For example, he does not understand that the potentialities of a thing, what it can do or become, depend on its nature but not on the external circumstances, and so *not* on the 'whole series of conditions'. His actualism is simply misconceived – a suggestion which gains support if we examine the logic of 'necessary conditions' which arguments like Hartmann's generally distort.

It is argued that if p is a necessary condition for q, and $\sim p$, then q is impossible. Yet it is an elementary point that what follows from these premises (it follows 'necessarily' of course, but that is another matter) is not that q is impossible, but merely that $\sim q$. What is impossible is q without p, but to assert this is merely to reiterate the major premiss. The *real* impossibility of q ('in the strict sense', we might add) is something that cannot be deduced simply from the absence of a 'necessary condition' for q. For to say that q is impossible without p is like saying that under no circumstances would q and $\sim p$ be the case, which is by no means the same thing as that q is impossible, or that under no circumstances would q be the case. If I falsely assert that my cat flew like a bird yesterday, the event I describe was impossible because it would not have happened under any circumstances. But if I equally falsely assert that the cat died yesterday, this event was not impossible, although, no doubt, some 'necessary condition' for the cat's demise was not fulfilled, because in certain circumstances it would have happened. For example, if the cat had been run over, or had eaten poison.

As this example can be taken to indicate, every assertion that it is a natural possibility (or impossibility, or necessity) that p, presupposes some kind of distinction between what p is about and, on the other hand, the 'surrounding circumstances'. In the special case of attributions of potentialities – what we have called 'natural powers' – the 'circumstances' comprise what lies 'outside' the nature of the agent. But a similar explanation seems applicable whenever a particular event is identified and is said to be possible or impossible, although it may be out of place to talk of 'power' or 'potentiality'. If we say of a patient under an anaesthetic that it is impossible that he should feel pain,[1] we imply that (in this situation) he would not feel pain 'in any circumstances'. We should not, of course, count the supposition of his not being anaesthetised as a 'circumstance'. We should not be refuted by the absurd argument that the event that we described as impossible actually took place soon afterwards, when the effects of the drug had predictably worn off. We were talking about *that* situation, in which the patient was drugged. But the other side to this penny is that the situation must be conceived of as limited by some boundary, beyond which other suppositions would fall. We can reasonably protest that we did not mean that the patient would not have felt pain even if he had not been drugged, but it would be unreasonable to deny that we implied that he would not have felt a jab with a pin. Otherwise why did

[1] Not, 'impossible that he is feeling pain', which simply means '*certain* that he is not'.

we talk of impossibility, rather than simply saying that the patient did not actually feel pain? The difference between the two suppositions, that of the patient's being conscious and that of his being jabbed with a pin, is that the former envisages an intrinsic difference in the situation we were talking about, while the latter would count as an extrinsic circumstance. Without such a distinction between situation and circumstance talk of possibility would be chimerical, and it is not surprising that philosophers who fail to recognise one reach paradoxical conclusions.

The problem we are considering is partly the problem of how it is possible to make particular possibility statements. In the case of universal possibility statements, 'It is possible for an A to be B', there is no problem about what to count as an extrinsic circumstance: provided that a thing is A, all other factors are 'circumstances' and whatever these may be, if the thing is also B, it is an instance that confirms the possibility-statement. But in the case of 'It is possible for *that* to be B' the problem arises of how much to include in the nature of the thing or situation referred to, and what to count as 'the circumstances'. This is not a problem we encounter in everyday life. We do not normally wonder whether to allow that a wreck without an engine or wheels can do 100 m.p.h., on the ground that, if it had been entirely rebuilt and suitably driven, it would have done 100 m.p.h. There is no doubt that it now cannot do 100 m.p.h., even though, if it were rebuilt, it then could. The problem is a philosophical problem, and I have tried to sketch a reasonable answer. The actualist gives an unreasonable answer, lacking in a sense of reality.

Not surprisingly, our problem is related to a well-known problem about particular hypotheticals. To assert that if anyone touches a red-hot poker, he will get burnt, is to assert a universal proposition which is obviously not refuted if we get a red-hot poker, cool it, and then touch it without getting burnt. But would this constitute a refutation if it had been asserted that if anyone touches *this* poker, he will get burnt? We have produced p without q, so it might seem that 'if p, then q' is refuted. But this conclusion is absurd, and common sense tells us that, since the hypothetical assertion was originally made when the poker was red-hot, it was true; even if, now that the situation is changed, it is no longer true that if you touch the poker, it will burn you.

The mistaken objection might here be put, that, if it is *ever* possible to plead that the situation has changed, it is *always* possible to put forward such a defence. For in any test of a hypothetical assertion, the fulfilment of the antecedent will never be the *only* thing to have happened since the assertion was made. A similar, absurd argument applies to possibility: if I say that it is impossible that this red-hot poker should be bent and someone picks up the poker in order to prove me wrong, I might claim that the situation is now an entirely different one, since I was talking about the situation before the poker was picked up and put under stress. This kind of argument has the unacceptable implication that it is impossible ever to test hypotheticals or possibility-statements. In both cases we need to understand that it is reasonable to draw a distinction between changes that are changes in the situation and those that are not. In other words, it is an essential aspect of both kinds of statement that they are theoretically testable.

It is important to recognise that the distinction, when it exists, is not arbitrary. A widespread theory is that particular hypotheticals and possibility-statements are really disguised, generally *elliptical* universal statements: that the distinction between 'situation' and 'circumstance' is a function of what the speaker leaves out but, presumably, has in mind. The obvious objection to this is that I might mean by 'If this switch is moved, the lights will go on' exactly what an electrician means, and yet he be in a better position to say what would constitute a change in the 'situation'. Such a statement is obviously not elliptical, and the speaker need have no further specification of the 'situation' in mind ('provided the wire is not cut', etc.). This is because it is always more reasonable to draw the line in some places rather than others, when we know the facts.

Actualism breeds on such confusions. The familiar metaphysical assertions that everything happens necessarily, and that the present total state of the universe, in virtue of some preceding total state, could not but have occurred, are extreme formulations which most clearly preclude the possibility of our distinction – for what would be the 'circumstances' in which a sequence of 'states of the universe' occurs? – and so conflict with the correct Millian interpretation of necessity as 'that which will be, whatever supposition we may make in regard to all other things'. These metaphysical assertions, that is to say, have a characteristic that renders them in principle unverifiable by the methods appropriate to the verification of assertions that something is impossible. Alternatively, perhaps, they can be regarded simply as false. For if the normal relevance of contrary-to-fact suppositions is allowed, the supposition that we must first allow is that the preceding state of the universe was not after all everything, was not the total state of the universe. It would then be easy to mention conditions in which the present state of affairs would not have occurred.

There is more to be said. G. E. Moore, for example, thought that there is a clear answer to the question at issue: 'Obviously all that follows [from the assumption of universal causation] is that, in *one* sense of the word "could", nothing ever *could* have happened, except what did happen. This really *does* follow.' The suggestion I am putting forward is that such a conclusion may be senseless, and in any case, does not follow. Against this suggestion it may be argued that the assertion that the present state of the universe could not but have occurred has, like its contradictory, a clear meaning, and is in principal verifiable: it means that everything that is happening has a cause, or is 'determined', and its contradictory means that some things are 'indetermined'. The word 'can', it may be said, simply provides a handy and intelligible and natural way of marking this distinction. There is no rule of language, written or unwritten, which forbids its use.

An example that is sometimes raised is that of statistical laws. If we regard it as simply the most probable result of the random movement of particles that gases at rest exert a uniform pressure in all directions, then it would not be absolutely contrary to the laws by which we explain its behaviour if the air in my room were suddenly to raise a book to the ceiling, by an exceedingly unlikely concatenation of events. Are we not therefore entitled to describe this event as a 'possibility', and even to ascribe to the air the 'potentiality' or 'power' of doing such a thing? Yet this 'power' could not be analysed in terms of what would happen in some circumstances, since its actualisation is envisaged as a result of chance, not of circumstances. In the same way, a world in which there was indeterminacy could be said to contain unactualised 'potentialities' of a kind not contained in a world in which there was no indeterminacy.

Moore would presumably have accepted this argument, since it explains his '*one* sense of the word "could" '. We may suppose that he would then have pointed out that such a sense is not the usual sense, and that this is just what is overlooked by the philosophical determinist. It is in fact hard to see how it could be proved that there is a positive linguistic error involved in the choice of the language of 'possibility' and 'potentiality' to express the empirical theory of scientific determinism or its contradictory. The words are there to be used, so to speak, and provided that they are successful, that is enough. Moreover, as we shall see later on, it is probably incorrect to multiply, as Moore does, different senses of 'can' and 'possible'. Nevertheless, Moore is nearly enough on the right lines for this to be no defence for the metaphysical determinist or 'actualist' against our previous remarks. The whole claim of actualism is that the fact (if it is a fact) of 'universal causation' should be seen to have sweeping consequences for our ordinary talk of potentiality. The actualist claims to draw, from an acceptable premiss, the conclusion that we are wrong ever to suppose that it is 'really possible' that the cat should have died, when it did not, or to suppose that this car could have done 100 m.p.h. when it only did 50 m.p.h., or that it could have done no more than 50 m.p.h. when it actually did 100 m.p.h. The actualist is convinced that, when he asserts that nothing can act otherwise than it does, he is saying just the same kind of thing as is meant by the categorical assertion that a car cannot travel at a certain speed. This conviction springs from one source, a thoroughgoing misunderstanding of what it is to ascribe a potentiality to something, or to say that, in a particular situation, something is possible. Once this misunderstanding is removed, most of the motive is also removed for describing a world in which everything has a cause, as one in which 'nothing ever could have happened, except what did happen'.

5. THE REFUTATION OF THE THEORY THAT 'ALL POWER IS CONDITIONAL'

We shall spend a little more time considering how the philosophical determinist arrives at his distorted picture of natural possibility, and how he is able to present it in a plausible light. Here I might make the point very strongly that it is never my purpose to defend 'ordinary language'. At present it is the last thing I want to do, since the determinist borrows his rhetoric from just this source, and it is we who must plead for 'strict speaking', or at any rate for a more careful and sensible interpretation of loose speaking.

The actualist is prepared to argue that a match that is not being struck is not capable of making a light. A remonstrance on behalf of the custom of attributing powers to unstruck and unlit matches is likely to be met with the claim that determinism is simply the general statement of what everyone at other times accepts, namely that a match cannot make a light unless it is struck (especially if it is a safety match), cars cannot do 100 m.p.h. if their engines are switched off, and water cannot boil unless it is heated. The only consolation allowed to us is that maybe the match *could* make a light, *if* it were struck. If we persist in opposing the paradoxical claim that it is never true to say of any water that it is capable of boiling, unless it actually is boiling, we appear to be committing ourselves to the indeed ridiculous position that it is possible to boil cold water without heating it.

This is the line of argument taken up by Hobbes, who contends that all powers possessed by particular things are conditional, in that the 'agent' does not have 'active power' unless it is applied to the appropriate 'patient', nor a patient 'passive power' unless it is applied to an appropriate agent. The only unconditional power, according to him, is what he calls 'plenary power', which is a combination of the power of the agent to act and the power of the patient to be acted upon. But this 'power', which incidentally does not seem to *belong* to anything but simply to exist, is such that, if it exists, the action will actually take place. 'Every act, therefore, which is possible shall at some time be produced.' (*Elements of Philosophy*, Ch X.) Consistency really demands from him, of course, the extreme actualist conclusion that every act which is possible is now being produced. Hobbes' argument is in formal terms, but it puts us in the same quandary as before. For if we assert in opposition to it that an 'agent' may have the power to act even when it is not applied to an appropriate 'patient', thinking of the match lying in the match-box, which is capable of starting a fire, we seem to be denying that it is a necessary condition of the action's actually taking place that the agent should be applied to an appropriate patient, as if the match could actually start a fire without being struck and applied to some combustible material. But are we really committed to contradicting whatever would normally be meant by 'This match cannot start a fire unless it is struck'? It does not seem that we are.

Let us consider this sentence, together with others like it, e.g., 'This car could do 100 m.p.h., only if there were petrol in the tank', 'This match could start a fire, if there were something to burn', 'This car can do 100 m.p.h., provided that the accelerator is fully depressed.' It is in fact easy to imagine that each of these sentences should express truths, on some occasions of their use. But on my own theory of potentiality, it might seem impossible that they should do so. For of the necessary conditions for the actualisation of the power, only those that are 'intrinsic', according to this theory, are also necessary conditions for the existence of the power. Powers are a matter of the nature of their possessor, and are not dependent on the circumstances in which their possessor is placed. Yet the present examples might all seem to imply some sort of dependence of the power, *per impossibile*, on 'extrinsic' factors. We can, however, avoid such a paradox, by recognising that these statements, on their natural interpretation, are not genuinely 'conditional' statements at all, but are to be explained in some other way. Fortunately it is easy to substantiate this suggestion.

It can hardly be denied that there is a very striking difference between the statement that this car could have done 100 m.p.h., if the accelerator had been fully depressed, and the statement that it could have done 100 m.p.h., if it had been a Rolls-Royce, or if it had had a new engine. The difference, surely, is that whereas the second statement does not imply that the car was capable of doing 100 m.p.h. (and even suggests that it could not), we can conclude from the first that the car really was capable of doing 100 m.p.h. No genuine conditional implies its own consequent – how could it? It is therefore reasonable to regard the first statement as a pseudo-conditional, which our determinist has mistaken for a genuine hypothetical like the second statement.

The statement that this car *cannot* do 100 m.p.h. *unless* the accelerator is depressed, is also other than it seems, and is different in kind from the statement that it cannot do 100 m.p.h. unless the engine has been replaced. It looks as if it would be correct to infer from the former, together with 'The accelerator is not depressed', the conclusion 'The car cannot do 100 m.p.h.', which is what can be inferred from the latter together with the premiss 'The engine has not been replaced.' But this appearance is deceptive, for the first statement is like 'It is not poisonous unless you eat it', while the second is like 'It is not poisonous unless it contains arsenic'. And berries that are only poisonous if eaten are also poisonous on the bush. A soporific is a soporific on the shelf, not only when taken after meals, and the fact that it may be intelligible, idiomatic and true to say that 'It is soporific only if taken after meals' does not prove the contrary. For this is a pseudo-conditional. So too is 'It would have been poisonous, if it had been taken after a heavy meal (but, as it is, you're safe).' The statement that it would have been poisonous, if it had been arsenic, is obviously very different.

It is tempting to offer, as a simple explanation for the fact that some apparently conditional statements are not genuinely so, the theory that, supposing 'ϕ' to stand for any predicate attributing a power or dispositional property to the subject, then 'x is ϕ' can always be analysed as a hypothetical, 'if x is P, then x will be Q', where P and Q are non-dispositional predicates. For in that case 'If x is P, then x will be ϕ' could not easily be taken as a genuine hypothetical. If 'x is fragile' means 'If x is dropped, x will break', then 'x is fragile, if dropped' (unless it is a peculiar way of saying that x will break, if dropped twice) collapses into 'If x is dropped, it will break', i.e. into its own consequent, 'x is fragile'. According to such an argument, our pseudo-hypotheticals, having as consequents 'x is ϕ', cannot be genuine hypotheticals, in virtue of the *meaning* of ϕ.[1]

This argument is much too simple for our purposes, however. It cannot plausibly be claimed that the reason why 'It could do 100 m.p.h., if the accelerator were depressed (if it were in top gear, etc.)' is not a genuine conditional, is entirely because of the meaning of 'It can do 100 m.p.h.' For it is obviously not necessary to refer specifically to accelerators, gears and so on in order to give the meaning of the latter. That is the point of giving an 'unspecific' hypothetical, 'In some circumstances, p', as a paraphrase of 'p is possible'. According

---

[1] It is interesting that although 'if x is dropped, x is fragile' would be a queer 'consequential' conditional, it might be an acceptable 'inferential' conditional, following from, e.g., 'Only fragile things are dropped.' Cf. p. 81 above. This, of course, is no good to the determinist.

to my own account, the distinction between genuine and pseudo-conditionals must rest on the intrinsic – extrinsic distinction. But this, as we have said, is an empirical distinction, not *a priori*. I might therefore be faced with the objection, not merely that the explanation of 'pseudo-hypotheticals' given in the last paragraph is too glib, but that I am now committed to the impossible task of explaining an allegedly logical, *a priori* distinction between classes of statement, by means of an *a posteriori* difference; and that therefore the distinction between genuine and pseudo-conditionals cannot be maintained.

The trouble with my argument, as it stands, is that it neglects the fact that the meaning of a statement at least partly depends on the intention of the person who makes it. Perhaps someone – someone, for example, with a belief in magic – *could*, when he utters the sentence 'This match could start a fire, if there was something to burn', intend to imply that the power of the match is conditional on the presence of combustibles. Presumably the metaphysical determinist, in the throes of theorising, means just that; which is why he is wrong. On the other hand, anyone who utters this sort of sentence in ordinary life is normally well aware that by laying a fire we do not magically create a power in the match, and consequently he will not mean what he says as a genuine conditional. The mere fact that someone could mean by the same form of words that the fulfilment of the condition would bring about the existence of the power, as well as helping to bring about its actualisation, is not damaging. For we are concerned with the argument that determinism follows from truths that we all accept. And if we reflect on what we would normally understand by 'It is only capable of making a light, if it is struck', 'It is only poisonous if eaten after a heavy meal' and so on, as opposed to such statements as 'It can only make a light, if it is a match', or 'It is only poisonous, if it is arsenic', it should be clear enough that we would *not* allow the inferences 'It is not being struck; therefore it is not capable of making a light', or It is not being eaten after a heavy meal; therefore it is not poisonous.'

A pseudo-conditional, 'x can do a, if x is P', is simply an idiomatic way of asserting, not that something is a sufficient condition for the existence of the power, but that something is a necessary condition for the actualisation of the power which exists. If we want to test the power, this condition should be fulfilled. It is natural that we should often want to link, in the same breath, the assertion of a possibility with a specification of conditions for its actualisation; for if we say that in some circumstances such and such will happen, we are likely to be asked, or to want to add, in just what circumstances. It is simply unfortunate that the handy enough method we adopt lends itself to misconstruction in a philosophical context. But 'It can do 100 m.p.h.', as it occurs in 'It can do 100 m.p.h., provided that the accelerator is fully depressed', is normally no more a real, as opposed to a grammatical, consequent or apodosis, than it is in 'It can do 100 m.p.h., although it will not unless the accelerator is depressed.'

The distinction between pseudo-conditionals and real conditionals provides an answer to a general deterministic argument, but some instances can raise special problems for its application. Some we have mentioned in a related context. Are damp matches only conditionally capable of starting a fire (since they would only be capable, if they were dried out), or are they categorically, actually, capable (since they would start a fire if, among other things, they were dried out)? Perhaps this is merely a case near the borderline, but other examples seem to raise fresh problems. How am I to deal with the plausible suggestion that if a lorry, which is now heavily laden, cannot do 70 m.p.h. except when it is empty, then it now cannot do 70 m.p.h.? Being laden is surely an 'extrinsic' property: *ex hypothesi*, the load does not affect the nature of the lorry, although, of course, it could do so, e.g. by breaking a spring. It therefore seems to follow from my principles that there is something wrong with the conclusion that the lorry now cannot do 70 m.p.h.: either an eccentric construction is being placed upon the premiss, i.e. it is being taken as a genuine conditional, or else the inference is invalid. But is it quite wrong to say, in this case, that the lorry cannot now do 70 m.p.h.?

We might approach this question by allowing flexibility in the matter of the identification of the 'agent'. Perhaps we can think of the heavily-laden-lorry as a unified thing, in such a way that it is reasonable to take 'It could do 70 m.p.h., if it were not heavily laden' as a genuine conditional. But if we are talking about the powers of the lorry, *qua* lorry sometimes laden, sometimes empty, then the 'it' would have a different reference and we should understand such a statement as a pseudo-conditional, and accept that the lorry really can do 70 m.p.h.

A reason for disliking this approach is that it suggests that it is arbitrary what is considered as a 'thing'.

A less artificial and more widely applicable explanation is to recognise a hierarchy of 'actions' rather than of 'agents'. Uneasiness at dismissing the suggestion that our lorry cannot do 70 m.p.h. (because it is laden) is, no doubt, grounded in the fact that a lorry that can only do 70 m.p.h. if it is empty is less powerful than a lorry that can do 70 m.p.h. even when fully laden. Yet how are we to mark the difference in power between them if it is true to say categorically of them both that they can do the action in question, i.e. can do 70 m.p.h.? It seems helpful to suggest that we take the if-clause to modify, not the whole main clause, but simply the description of the action: doing 70-heavily-laden and doing-70-without-a-load are different performances, species, so to speak, of the genus 'doing 70'. Consequently, anything that can do one of the specific actions can, *ipso facto*, do the generic action, but if something cannot do a particular specific action, it does not follow that it cannot do the generic action. A car that can do 100 m.p.h. if it is going downhill, can do 100 m.p.h., even if it cannot do 100 m.p.h. uphill. Naturally, when it is going uphill, the question most likely to interest us has to do with the specific power it lacks, rather than the generic power it (categorically) possesses. Thus our heavily laden lorry can do 70 m.p.h., although (even when empty) it cannot do what may be needed now, which is to do 70 m.p.h. heavily laden.

A determinist might suggest that what is 'needed' or important at any time is the ability to do-the-action-in-the-present-state-of-the-universe; and argue that, if we thus precisely specify every action that is performed, it will be seen that the action never could have been performed on any occasion on which it was not performed. One thing wrong with this suggestion is that not every quasi-conditional clause mentioning a condition for the actualisation of a power can be treated as a further specification of the action that can be performed: e.g. 'This magnet can pick up pins, if there are any around.' The ability to pick up available pins is not a species of a generic ability to pick up pins, and it would be absurd to suggest that the ability to pick up non-available pins is ever called for. The present explanation is only appropriate, and only requisite, for a special class of cases.

6

The Powers of People and the Powers of Things

1. INTRODUCTORY

I shall now try to demonstrate that the power of a person to do an action is metaphysically or semantically different, in important ways, from the potentialities of a thing. In other words, the proposition that this man could have saved the drowning child is different in kind from the proposition that this drug could have cured the sick man. Success in establishing the difference will constitute a further objection to the commonest of deterministic lines of thought, the 'Basic Argument' of Chapter 1, which, in moving from premises about causally 'necessary conditions' for events to a conclusion about human abilities, depends upon smothering any such distinction under the enveloping folds of 'can'.

At the same time, there is the disappointing consequence that the long discussion of natural power, above, will not necessarily help to explicate the concept of personal power. I face in particular the formidable necessity of yet another explanation of 'the distinction betwixt power and its exercise'. Indeed, in the chapters following I must grope towards a fairly complete account of personal power and possibility for choice, if I am to answer the plausible argument that it differs from natural power and possibility precisely in that here there really is no foundation for a distinction between the possible and the actual. Yet we may hope that this disconcerting suggestion will already be less attractive, since our discussion so far should have taught us that those who grind the traditional axes in the freewill controversy are not necessarily the very best of guides to the concept of possibility.

2. THE DISTINCTION BETWEEN NATURAL AND PERSONAL POWER

Although no adequate account has ever been given of the difference between natural and personal power, not all philosophers have been unaware that such a distinction might exist. On the contrary, the orthodox 'libertarian' or indeterminist tends to argue very strongly that the powers of people must be seen as different from the powers of things. He is not satisfied with the consolation offered by some of the slightly less tough-minded determinists, which, roughly speaking, is that they do not mean to deny that trees often grow freely, stones often fall freely and men often act freely. Hobbes, for example, despite his rigorous actualism, allows men freedom of action in virtue of what he conceives of as the same sort of 'conditional power' as may be granted to things, but this salve simply elicits the scorn of his libertarian adversary, Bishop Bramhall: 'What! will he ascribe liberty to inanimate things also? . . . Judge then what a pretty kind of liberty it is which is maintained by T.H., . . . such a liberty as a river hath to descend down a channel.'[1] This is an entirely reasonable response, for the 'power to do otherwise' that relates to a man's 'liberty', responsibility, choice and the rest is indeed something different from the power of a motor-car to do other speeds than the speed it is doing at present, or from the capacity of an empty container.

Probably the most striking logical difference between the powers of a thing and a person's ability to do various particular actions is that the latter may depend very much on 'extrinsic' circumstances. A car that is locked in a garage does not thereby lose its powers, but a prisoner is deprived of some of his. When we ascribe a power to a thing we are characteristically saying something about its own nature but nothing about the circumstances in which it is placed; but if we assert that a man could have done an action we imply not only something about the man himself but also that the circumstances are favourable to the action, that there is nothing in them to prevent it.

Here we come upon the commonplace distinction between 'general capacity' and 'opportunity'. The general ability to read may be

[1] Hobbes and Bramhall: *Questions concerning Liberty*, etc., cf. Bradley: *Ethical Studies*, p. 25.

possessed by someone in circumstances that make reading impossible, while an illiterate in a library may have the opportunity but not the capacity. There is often, maybe, something a little odd in saying that someone 'has the opportunity' if he lacks the capacity. I should hardly describe my meeting a prize-fighter as a good opportunity for me to knock him down. But this seems to be a philosophically unimportant point of idiom, which in any case is not universal. For example, we talk of giving everyone an equal opportunity to get to the top, although we know that not everyone is capable of grasping it.

'Can' may be used to imply no more than the general capacity, and elsewhere perhaps no more than the opportunity ('In Miami you can swim in winter time'), but it is also often used to imply both. This, of course, is how we must take the phrase so dear to the hearts of the freewill controversialists, 'He could have acted otherwise', since an agent must at least have both the capacity and the opportunity to refrain from an action, if his doing it is to be the result of a free choice. Consequently, whereas if a thing stays the same and only its circumstances change, then its powers remain the same, what a man can do may vary considerably simply with the circumstances. This means that our analysis and explanation of natural possibility and power is not applicable to possibility for choice. 'He could have escaped' gives information about the prisoner's circumstances, and it would be absurd to assert that someone could have escaped, on the ground that in certain circumstances he would have escaped, for example if there had been no chains on his wrists. The chains are the reason why he could not escape.

We find this reflected in the reasonable interpretation of various 'could . . ., if . . .' statements. The statement that the pills in the cupboard could save the patient's life if he knew about them, implies that the pills are capable of saving the life. It cannot reasonably be interpreted as a genuine conditional, because how much the patient knows is not a fact about, nor can be supposed to affect, the nature and powers of the pills. But the same principle obviously does not apply to the statement that the doctor can save the patient's life, if the right pills are available (or, if his car does not break down, and so on,) which really is conditional. From 'He can only save her if the pills are available' and 'The pills are not available' we can deduce 'He is unable to save her', even though the availability of the pills can hardly be said to relate to the nature of the doctor. All of which confirms the intuition that the powers of people are different, but leaves the problem of finding another principle, perhaps another 'analysis', to explain the distinction between personal powers and their exercise, and to explain why they are not merely 'conditional', in Hobbes' sense.

We can imagine someone thinking that the argument of the last paragraphs leaves no way out but indeterminism, since it may suggest to him the following inappropriate model for understanding personal power. Imagine that a current of water is turning a mill-wheel and that the stream which is actually turning the wheel is capable of turning the millstone. That is to say, in certain circumstances it would do so; a suitable condition being, let us suppose, the pulling of a lever, causing the cogs on the mill-wheel to engage with the mechanism that works the millstone. Now the general capacity or capacities involved in a man's power to do an action on a particular occasion might seem to be just like the power of the stream to turn the millstone, which admittedly might exist even if other circumstances 'prevent', as we might say, its exercise. But we have seen that a person's power to do a particular action also involves opportunity, and it is tempting to look for the analogue for 'opportunity' in the inanimate activity. What else could be meant by 'giving the opportunity' to the stream to exercise its power, except the fulfilling of a condition, such as the pulling of the lever, in which it actually will turn the millstone? In fact it seems an unavoidable conclusion, if the stream is not turning the millstone, that either it is not being given the chance to demonstrate its strength, or else it is not after all powerful enough to do the task. In Hobbes' somewhat quaint terminology, either the active or the passive power must be absent. But if this represents an appropriate way of looking at capacity and opportunity, how do we avoid the conclusion that, if a man does not do an action, then either he lacks the capacity or he lacks the opportunity? And the corollary of this conclusion, that actions that are not performed could not be performed?

It might occur to someone in this dilemma that the only way to introduce the required flexibility is to postulate 'indeterminism', so that to attribute a general capacity to a person is never to say that in certain circumstances he definitely will do the action, but is to say that in certain circumstances he *might* do the action, although perhaps he might not, and to imply that this uncertainty is in the nature of things irremediable. Now in spite of all that is wrong with indeterminism, and the absolute rightness of the criticism that nothing whatsoever is gained towards demonstrating even the bare possibility of 'free choice', let alone knowledge that it exists, by a suggestion that attempts to explain it by relegating it to the realm of random, unpredictable and presumably ungovernable events, nevertheless the present suggestion is not entirely foolish. For at least this much is true, as a minimum of unprejudiced reflection will confirm: it really is impossible to predict simply from the fact that a man is capable of doing an action and also has the opportunity, that he will do it. But what is wrong with the deterministic model presented above is not that it neglects some presumption of randomness in human actions, but that it is a mistake to see in the powers of an inanimate object any sort of close logical analogue to the general capacities of a person, or to suppose that 'opportunity' is at all adequately explained if we assimilate it to the external circumstances that stimulate, or are requisite for, the actualisation of the physical potentialities of a thing. It is not the only difference between personal and natural power that the existence, as well as the exercise of the former depends on external circumstances. The logical situation is much more complicated than that.

3. THE REFUTATION OF RYLE'S DISPOSITIONALIST ACCOUNT OF HUMAN CAPACITIES

It is not only avowed determinists who are prepared to assimilate a man's ability to run at ten miles an hour with his car's power of doing sixty, and at this point we are likely to find ranged against us, not simply those who appear to have a vested interest in keeping the free-will pot boiling, but also many of those who adopt a more pacificatory approach and are eager enough to lower the temperature in this particular area. Perhaps their eagerness is too great, for in philosophy, as in society, extremism is not the only enemy of right thinking.

One of the most influential of recent discussions of the logical nature of human capacities occurs in Gilbert Ryle's *Concept of Mind*.

The cornerstone of his account is that capacities are 'dispositions', but before we can disagree with this we need to know what it means. At one point Ryle writes that 'merely to classify a word as signifying a disposition is not yet to say much more about it than that it is not used for an episode.'[1] Now the statements that we make about someone, when we say that he can swim, speak French, sing or do geometry, are certainly not descriptive of particular episodes or series of episodes in his life, and so would seem to be, in Ryle's sense, 'dispositional'. Yet Ryle is himself prepared, without more ado, to say something further about dispositions. He reproves those who 'ignore the ways in which dispositional concepts actually behave': 'Sentences embodying these dispositional words' are to be interpreted as 'testable, open hypothetical and what I shall call "semi-hypothetical" statements'.[2] He means that attributions of dispositional properties are *equivalent* to hypothetical statements of one sort or another, which is, of course, different from saying that they are themselves hypothetical.

It is evident that despite his sweeping suggestion that anything is a disposition which is not an episode, Ryle has very definite paradigms in mind. His archetypal dispositions are physical or natural 'dispositions', causal properties such as brittleness and solubility: 'to possess a dispositional property is not to be in a particular state, or to undergo a particular change; it is to be bound or liable to be in a particular state, or to undergo a particular change, when a particular condition is realised. The same is true about specifically human dispositions . . .' (op cit., p. 43). Among the specifically human dispositions are said to be human capacities and abilities, which are continually lumped together with such entities as propensities, habits, liabilities and bents. Just the same sort of account is given of both classes: we are told not only that 'To be brittle is just to be bound or likely to fly into fragments in such and such conditions; to be a smoker is just to be bound

---

[1] P. 116. It would be hypercritical to complain that this odd remark would make most of the words in the dictionary signify dispositions.

[2] Ryle does not of course mean by 'open hypothetical' statements what I have above called 'open' or 'unspecific' hypotheticals: i.e. 'In some circumstances, *p*'. He means, e.g., 'If (whenever) she sees blood, she faints', as opposed to 'If she had seen blood (then), she would have fainted.'

or likely to fill, light and draw on a pipe in such and such conditions', but also that 'To say that this sleeper knows [i.e. can speak and understand] French, is to say that if, for example, he is ever addressed in French, or shown any French newspaper, he responds pertinently in French, acts appropriately or translates it correctly into his own tongue.' (My parenthesis, in the spirit of Ryle.)

One thing that might set us on our guard is the conflict between Ryle's terminology and the language that is most natural. We do not normally talk of the 'dispositions' of inanimate objects, although this usage has a long tradition in philosophical jargon and is harmless enough. We do, however, readily attribute dispositions to people, but the term covers aspects of character and personality, never capacities or skills. To ascribe to someone a disposition of a certain sort, sunny, acquisitive or what have you, is not normally to say anything at all about his capabilities or his competences. Whatever the significance of this point of language, Ryle is himself uneasily aware that capacities, and 'can' in general, require some sort of special treatment. His efforts to give a satisfactory explanation that does not clash with his general picture of the 'dispositional' are unavailing but revealing.

One section, early in his book, is devoted to contrasting 'intelligent capacities' with 'habits'. Here we might expect to find a clue to the logical differences between saying of a man that he can perform some action and saying that he is in the habit of performing it, between the statement that he is capable of doing crosswords, and the statement that he does crosswords habitually. But Ryle's explanation of this contrast is largely in terms of the kind of action performed, or the way in which it is performed, as if this must differ according to whether it is the exercise of a capacity or a habit. An habitual action or, as he tendentiously puts it, an action done 'by pure or blind habit', is said to be done automatically, without thought, whereas one that is the exercise of a skill involves the agent in carefully thinking what he is doing. But it should be apparent that the general distinction between capacities, even intelligent capacities, and habits cannot be explained by a distinction between actions or modes of acting, since the same action may be a manifestation of both a capacity or skill and a habit. Of course, the habit of driving carefully and the habit of doing crosswords are not blind habits, but not all habits are blind. What Ryle promises, or seems to promise, is an account of the difference between skills and habits (*v.* p. 42, first paragraph).

A similar criticism seems applicable to Ryle's suggestion, in line with his account of 'heed' (Ch. V, section 4), that the question whether an action is an exercise of an intelligent capacity or of a 'mere' habit hangs not so much on the quality of the action itself as on its place in a series of actions: 'It is of the essence of merely habitual practices that one performance is a replica of its predecessors. It is of the essence of intelligent practices that one performance is modified by its predecessors.' The difference corresponds, he suggests, to the difference between 'drill' and 'training'. But again, if we regard doing a crossword as an action – and why not? – there seems no reason why it should not be habitual, even though it is true that, as a rule, no two crosswords done by the same person are identical, and nearly everyone gets better at crosswords, the more he does. It is also not clear why, even if the most striking manifestations of intelligence often involve an adaptation of behaviour to unusual circumstances, it nevertheless may not equally often be intelligent to do just what one has done before, however frequently. In any case, an intelligent practice is not the same as an intelligent capacity. The suspicion arises that Ryle's remarks, whether sound or not, are more relevant to the distinguishing features of capacities, practices and, for that matter, habits that are marks of intelligence, than to the logical distinction between habits and any kind of capacity. The latter distinction cannot be explained simply by a difference between types of action or activity.

There are other passages in which Ryle seems to claim credit for disclosing the specific nature of 'capacities' within the genus of 'dispositions', when he is really drawing attention to some quite unrelated distinction. In the same section, on intelligent capacities and habits, a 'further important difference' between them is said to consist in the fact that the former are not 'simple, single-track' dispositions, like brittleness or being a pipe-smoker, which manifest themselves in one kind of action only. It is characteristic of them, on the contrary, that their exercise is 'indefinitely heterogeneous' and may take 'a wide and perhaps unlimited variety of shapes'. Consequently, so it is said, we cannot give the meaning of the ascription of an intelligent capacity in the form of a straightforward hypothetical specifying just what the agent would do in such and such circumstances, as, according to Ryle, we can give the meaning of 'He's a pipe-smoker'. We must 'unpack' what is conveyed by these more 'complex' dispositional statements by means of 'an infinite series of different hypothetical propositions' (p. 44). In this respect 'intelligent capacities' are said to be like 'hardness', 'elasticity' and 'pride': 'there are several different reactions which we expect of an elastic object', while we cannot sum up someone's pride as 'just the tendency to do this, whenever a situation of that sort arose'. Such concepts are 'highly generic', 'determinable', 'complex', 'vague', while others are 'specific', 'determinate', 'simple', 'precise'. These expressions and examples are culled from the various places in the book in which Ryle discusses the distinction.

The trouble with this contrast is not that it has no foundation (although it is perhaps not entirely clear what this is, or how important it is) but that it will not do any of the work Ryle tries to get from it. It cannot account for, because it cuts right across, the distinction between capacities on the one hand and dispositions or habits on the other, as his own examples of 'determinable' concepts admirably demonstrate. Moreover, so far as its actualisation goes, the ability to scratch the back of one's head is exactly as 'determinate' as the habit of scratching the back of one's head. Nor is it a necessary feature of an intelligent capacity that it should be 'determinable'. Intelligence itself and the ability to reason are no doubt generic enough, but the ability to construct mathematical proofs is less so, while the ability to construct a proof of Pythagoras' Theorem or to add 295 to 2672 is highly specific. Habits too can be more or less determinate: compare the habit of being polite with the habit of raising one's hat to ladies, or to one particular lady. The hierarchy of genus and species, or of determinable and determinate, can throw no light on the logic of personal capacities, or on that of intellectual capacities in particular.

In a later chapter (Ch. V, Sect. 3: 'Mental Capacities and Tendencies') Ryle conducts an extended and frontal attack on the problem at its most general, introducing the theory, which, incidentally, conflicts with his earlier remarks about capacities, that there is something *negative* about 'can': that to attribute a capacity to someone is essentially to make a hypothetical statement, but a negative one. He invites us to consider how we should colloquially express the contradictory of 'If I walk under the ladder, I shall meet trouble during the day', and suggests that we should be prepared to put it, 'I could walk under it without having trouble', or, more generally, 'Trouble does not necessarily come to people who walk under ladders'. Consequently, there is 'only a stylistic difference between the if-then idiom and the modal forms'. Ryle expressly excepts some uses of 'can' (e.g. the permissive 'You can get up now'), but he takes it that the single 'ladder' example demonstrates the point as far as capacities are concerned.

The only case in which Ryle attempts explicitly to break down a 'can' into a 'not if-then' is a significantly peculiar one.[1] For one thing, the 'could' is eminently *not* being used in 'I could walk under the ladder without meeting trouble' in order to attribute a capacity, or anything like a skill, ability or competence. The statement is merely to the effect that trouble would not follow causally, or 'necessarily' in the train of my action. The absence of trouble, if it did not occur, need not be due to the exercise of some power or capability of mine. It may be noticed that 'I walked under the ladder without meeting trouble later' is not a more detailed description of the action of walking under the ladder, like 'I walked without stumbling'; nor is my escaping trouble conceived of as an activity like, say, avoiding puddles. It might be said that the admission of walking-without-stumbling as an action and of the ability to walk without stumbling as an accomplishment supports Ryle, since he might have chosen an example involving such a genuine action. But in fact it is pretty clear that 'I am capable of walking without stumbling' is *not* the contradictory of 'If I walk, I stumble.' For we can conjoin the two without a suspicion of self-contradiction, as readily as we can say, 'Although she can (or could) knit without looking, yet if she knits she looks.' Of course, if I cannot walk without stumbling, then if I walk, I stumble; and if the girl cannot knit without looking, then if she is knitting, she is looking. But such one-way entailments are palpably insufficient for Ryle's equation.

In fact, Ryle's own example is very much like a 'natural possibility'

[1] Another example in which the break-down is implied (i.e. 'Fido can howl when the moon shines' = 'It is not true that if the moon shines, Fido is silent': op. cit., p. 131) has the same peculiarities, which are even more evidently present simply in order to preserve the theory: 'when the moon shines' is entirely gratuitous. Why doesn't Ryle discuss the proposition that Fido can howl, full stop?

statement. It is worth noting, but is hardly surprising, that 'can' may be used with a personal subject to express such propositions. 'The healthiest child could catch cold' (even, '... is capable of catching') is another example, which we may roughly construe as 'In some circumstances, the healthiest child will (would) catch cold', or perhaps as Ryle's negative hypothetical, not much different, 'It is not the case that if a child is very healthy he will not catch cold.' It is in precisely this respect that it *differs* from the natural interpretation of 'The cleverest child is capable of answering all the questions.' It might be added that Ryle's analysis has a feature that seems to make it inadequate even for all natural possibility-statements. To have what we have called a 'specific' hypothetical, in which the condition is specified, there must be two specific predicates: in his example, these are 'walk under a ladder' and 'meet trouble'. But two such predicates cannot be derived from 'This can do 100 m.p.h.', nor, for that matter, from 'This engine necessarily makes a noise.'

Ryle has more to say about capacities and tendencies, but nothing which supports his main contention as to the difference between them. One prominent paragraph claims that:

> Tendencies are different from capacities and liabilities. 'Would if . . .' differs from 'could'; and 'regularly does . . . when . . .' differs from 'can'. Roughly, to say 'can' is to say that it is not a certainty that something will not be the case, while, to say 'tends', 'keeps on' or 'is prone', is to say that it is a good bet that it will be, or was, the case. So 'tends to' implies 'can' but is not implied by it.

But this gloss on the central theory simply follows in the wake of Hume's confusion between certainty and necessity, which he too combined with the view that personal power consists in the possibility that it will be exercised. We may notice the oddity of lumping 'liabilities' in with 'capacities', when 'is liable to' seems in general much more like 'tends to', than like 'can'; but this move on Ryle's part springs from yet another effort to explain 'capacities', an effort which in some ways, perhaps, is the most interesting of all.

We can understand the special flavour of the 'can' that attributes a general capacity or competence, he suggests, if we recognise that 'we often say of a person that he can do something, in the sense that he can do it well'. Someone who cannot tell the time, tie reef-knots or spell *correctly*, cannot really do these things at all. It might be objected that this tells us more about the concept of telling the time than about a sense of 'can', but this is a point that Ryle seems prepared to take, and indeed to stress. For he goes on to suggest that it is when 'can' is combined with a verb of one kind that we have a 'capacity-expression', and when the verb is of a different kind we have a 'liability-expression'. The two kinds of verb are, respectively, what he calls 'verbs of success' and 'verbs of failure': e.g. 'hit', 'find', 'win', 'solve', 'cure', 'arrive', as opposed to 'miss', 'lose', 'misspell', 'miscalculate' and so on.

The point of Ryle's argument is not, perhaps, entirely clear, but it seems to be connected with the following. We need only to contemplate certain groups of sentences including 'can' or 'capable' in order to be aware that, in their most natural interpretation, they fall into two classes: for example, 'he can drive', 'she is capable of adding up', 'he cannot dance' fall into one class, whereas '(Even) she is capable of making a mistake', 'He *can* drive badly (sometimes)' and 'She was incapable of putting a foot wrong (even once)' fall into another class. The entirely justifiable suspicion arises that here we have statements of a different logical structure, so that any uniform or general theory, such as Ryle's, is unlikely to cover both. This suspicion is confirmed when we reflect on such examples as 'She is capable of saying cleverer things than he, although she takes care never to do so', which makes impeccable and self-consistent sense, while '(Even) she is capable of making a mistake, although she takes care never to do so', on the contrary, is self-contradictory, like saying both that you cannot and that you can rely on her not to make a mistake. Ryle, however, while conceding that there is a difference, and even going so far as to talk of different *senses* of 'can', attempts to explain it in such a way as not to upset his single general account of possibility. The different flavour of the 'can' arises, he suggests, just because, and in so far as, being capable of doing something right is an asset,[1] whereas being 'capable' of bungling something is not. Hence we think of the former as a competence or capability, and of the latter as a liability. We describe one person as competent at spelling, another as liable to make mistakes.

[1] Ryle does not use the word 'asset'. Unless I completely misunderstand him, it contains his thought.

This ingenious explanation is wholly inadequate and almost wholly misleading, but I shall suggest that it contains a grain of truth. First, however, I shall try to explain what is wrong with it. We can allow that only if someone is capable of doing an action not incompetently are we likely to talk of a competence, and that by his 'abilities' we generally mean those abilities in which he excels, and that are useful to him. But this point is quite trivial. It is evident, and Ryle himself concedes,[1] that his discussion of competences and 'success-words' cannot explain the flavour of *every* 'can' that, unlike 'can make mistakes', attributes a real capacity to someone. 'Can walk' does not mean 'can walk well'. But in that case has Ryle done anything towards explaining what a real capacity is? Moreover, like his earlier and otherwise very different remarks on intelligent capacities *versus* habits, his explanation hinges on a distinction between the kinds of action or performance involved, and so is vulnerable to the same criticism that it cannot possibly explain a difference between cases in which the performance is the same: for example between saying of someone that he can made a noise exactly like a goat (at will), and saying that he is liable to make a noise exactly like a goat (at awkward moments), both of which may be expressed 'He is capable of making a noise exactly like a goat.' It is evident that Ryle is confusing these. That there is a logical difference is shewn by the fact that someone who is (really) capable of imitating a goat may not be in the least liable to do so, being, let us suppose, too well bred. This is the sort of crucial difference about which Ryle's special explanations of capacities, numerous and various as they are, are all merely evasive. It is easy to understand why, if we recognise that these explanations all have the purpose of bolstering up his incorrect general theory: namely that, when all is said and done, ascribing a power is always a matter of asserting or, as he sometimes suggests, denying that the subject would behave in a certain way if placed in a certain situation. It is central to Ryle's theme that human capacities, like all human 'dispositions', possess, beneath any surface peculiarity, essentially the same logical structure as the powers and dispositions, or 'causal properties' of things. But that is just what is

[1] Op. cit., p. 133. The earlier passage, however, in which the argument is presented, contains (I think) the different suggestion that more is accomplished by it than the identification of a mere sub-class of capacities.

THE POWERS OF PEOPLE AND THE POWERS OF THINGS 115

in dispute. We cannot say of an object that it is brittle, or of a substance that it is soluble, without implying that in certain circumstances, in certain favourable conditions, the object would break, the substance would dissolve. But we can truly say of a man that he is clever, or that he can speak French, or that he is capable of lifting his right arm, even if he would *under no circumstances* give correct answers to examiners (whom he prefers to deceive), or reply to Frenchmen (whom he despises) or raise his arm (which is against his religion). It is possible to refuse consistently to exercise a capacity.

It must be admitted that it is an unusual person who would be so obstinate or consistent about something as trivial as raising an arm, but the oddity of the case is contingent and the logical point simply follows from what was referred to at the end of the last section. If we know the potentiality of water, and know that the circumstances in which some water is placed are favourable and appropriate for the actualisation of that potentiality, then we can predict or infer its actualisation. We know that the kettle on the hearth will boil. But it is not enough to know, say, that a schoolboy is capable of raising his hand, and that the circumstances are, in themselves, perfectly favourable and even appropriate for this action, in order to have adequate grounds for a prediction that he will raise his hand. All sorts of other factors may be relevant: is he co-operative or contrary, exhibitionist or shy, cognizant or ignorant of the answer to the question asked, in a good mood or a bad one, or, for that matter, awake or asleep? Ignorance of these factors would not be ignorance of the 'surrounding circumstances', nor ignorance of the capacity in question, nor ignorance as to what circumstances constitute favourable or appropriate conditions for the exercise of the capacity, but ignorance of other aspects of the boy himself.

Perhaps it will help to refer to a very popular analysis of personal power, which I shall soon discuss in detail. That is the theory that 'I could . . .' means 'I would . . ., if I wished (chose, etc.).' While it is, in cold blood and without the subtle elaboration that Ryle provides, extremely implausible to say that the statement that a man has the power to raise his hand means that in certain external circumstances he would raise it, for example, that he would raise it if called upon to do so, it is much more plausible that it means that he would raise it if called upon to do so and if he were obedient, or that he would raise it if the circumstances were right and he had the motive or desire to raise it. But this second view is contrary to Ryle's general theory, and strikes at the heart of the comparison with causal properties. For motives, traits of character, desires and the rest are not 'surrounding circumstances' like the strikings, strainings, droppings and plungings into acid or water that appear in philosophical explanations of 'dispositions' such as brittleness and solubility.

A curious fact is that this difference goes unnoticed by philosophers who are prepared to incorporate the more plausible analysis into an argument *for* the view that personal capacities are veritable dispositions. At one point even Ryle himself makes the shift from his general theory, apparently without a qualm: 'To say that [a child] can tie a reef-knot is to say . . . that reef-knots are produced whenever, or nearly whenever, reef-knots are required, or at least that they are nearly always produced when required *and when the child is trying*' (my italics). In this single passage a theory of a quite different *type*, inconsistent with the main line of argument, is introduced as an afterthought. The same mistake is made by another influential writer, P. Nowell-Smith, even though he elsewhere offers some criticisms of Ryle:

> Capacities are a sub-class of dispositions. To say that a man 'can' do something is not to say that he ever has or will; there may be special reasons why the capacity is never exercised, for example that the occasion for exercising it has never arisen. A man might go through his whole life without ever adding 15 and 16; and we should not have to say that he couldn't do this. Yet a man cannot be said to be able to do something if all the necessary conditions are fulfilled and he has a motive for doing it (*sic*). It is logically odd to say 'Smith can run a mile, has had several opportunities, is passionately fond of running, has no medical or other reasons for not doing so, but never has in fact done so.' And, if it is true that this is logically odd, it follows that 'can' is equivalent to 'will . . . if . . .' and 'could have' to 'would have . . . if . . .' (*Ethics*, p. 277).

Now a 'passionate fondness for running' is not an extrinsic circumstance, but is itself, presumably, a 'disposition' of Smith. Nowell-

Smith himself tells us that 'fond of' is 'always used in a dispositional way' (op. cit., p. 129). Consequently, even if the suggested analysis into hypotheticals of 'Smith can run a mile' were correct, the conclusion that capacities are a sub-class of dispositions would fail to follow, for there are hypotheticals and hypotheticals. Moreover, as we shall later discover to the special embarrassment of this particular theory, there are some values of p and q such that '$s = if\ p,\ then\ q$' seems rather to be a reason for denying, than a reason for asserting that s is 'dispositional'.

Finally, what about the grain of truth in Ryle's attempt to base the distinction between capacities and liabilities on a contrast between doing something well and doing it badly, between success-verbs and failure-verbs? Why should 'can', if followed by a success-verb, attribute a capacity, but not if it is followed by a failure-verb? First of all, this is not universally true. What is true is that a real personal capacity is always a capacity to do an *action*, or at any rate to carry on an activity. What an 'action' is, in this context, may be a big question, but it is at least something conceived of as possibly intended or deliberate. There is something intrinsically inappropriate about words like 'mistake' or 'miscalculate' for the description of actions *qua* deliberate actions. A deliberate mistake, it seems, is no mistake. We can intentionally write down the wrong answer, but is this miscalculation? It is for this reason that 'can make a mistake' is inappropriate for the ascription of a real capacity.

But we may notice that Ryle's list of 'failure-verbs' has a place for some things which, although normally unintentional slips, may perfectly well be done deliberately: for example, misspelling or mispronouncing. Consequently the ability to misspell or mispronounce may be a real ability. Perhaps it is true that 'can misspell', 'is capable of misspelling' will more often than not mean simply 'is liable to misspell', as in 'Despite her education, she is capable of misspelling common words': but this seems to be because it is normally as pointless as it is easy to misspell a word deliberately, and so it is also normally pointless, but not false or logically absurd, to attribute to someone the ability to misspell words. Feats of misspelling might, of course, be difficult. It certainly requires concentration in order to misspell every four-letter word one uses.

'Success-verbs' are especially *appropriate* for describing deliberate actions. Hits, wins, cures, solutions and the rest are naturally conceived of as the outcome of intentional activity. 'Can hit', 'is capable of winning' and so on, therefore commonly attribute real capacities or abilities. Not, indeed, universally or necessarily. For one thing, successes may be due to luck, as elsewhere Ryle himself reminds us. Winning a lottery, which is the epitome of something that happens to people rather than something they do, cannot constitute the exercise of a true ability. Consequently 'He is capable of winning the lottery', unless it is used in the sense in which only people with tickets are capable of winning, will have much the same tone as 'He is capable of accidentally running over a policeman', or, for that matter, as the extravagant 'It is quite capable of raining on Bank Holiday.' But in any case, the point of a 'can' or 'is capable' may not be to ascribe an ability or competence even when what follows is an unimpeachable deliberate action; as when we accuse the boor of being capable of singing in his bath. It is a necessary condition for a capacity's being a *real* capacity or ability that it should be the capacity to do an action. But it is not a sufficient condition, and so this truism does not take us very far in distinguishing the peculiar 'can' of personal power.

7

Ifs and Cans

1. INTRODUCTORY

I have already mentioned theories that the 'can' of personal power is analysable by means of hypotheticals, the subordinate clauses of which bring in a reference to such things as motives, fondnesses and efforts. I shall now subject these analyses to a critical examination and, for a variety of reasons, reject them. I shall show that attributions of personal power have verificational peculiarities that no such theory can account for. First, however, I shall turn to another closely related suggestion which probably needs to be considered if we are to understand the currently orthodox opinion. This other view is the familiar doctrine, now applied to personal power, that 'all power is conditional': i.e. that when it is said that a man was capable of doing something that he did not actually do, the assertion can only be true if what is really meant is that he could have done it if some condition, which was not actually fulfilled, had been fulfilled.

I make no apology for borrowing the title of J. L. Austin's address to the British Academy for the title of my own discussion. While it would indeed be difficult to match his originality and penetration, he has made it as hard to think of the present subject except as 'Ifs and Cans'.[1]

2. THE REFUTATION OF THE THEORY THAT ALL PERSONAL POWER IS CONDITIONAL

Like the parallel theory about natural power, the fallacious doctrine that all personal power is conditional can be represented in a way that

---

[1] Reprinted in J. L. Austin: *Philosophical Papers*.

makes it immediately attractive and compelling, just because there is an idiomatic form of words available that looks as if it expressed a conditional, logically weaker than the categorical assertion, but such that it is difficult to dissent from the suggestion that it is 'all we mean' when we attribute powers categorically. When we say of a match that it was capable of starting a fire although it did not, we are told that we surely do not mean to assert more than that it *could* have done so, *if* it had been struck – but then it was not struck, and so was not, strictly speaking, capable of starting a fire.[1] Similarly, if we say that someone was capable of doing something that he omitted doing, we may be told that we must surely mean that he *could* have done it, *if* he had chosen to (or wished to, or tried to, or something similar). How can I deny that by 'I could have moved my finger' I do not normally mean any more than that I could have moved it, if I had chosen to? In that case, we shall be told, I am not making any claim about what I was actually capable of doing, and in fact I could *only* have moved it *if* I had chosen.

Although this argument may seem to be just another attempt to demonstrate that metaphysical determinism follows from what we all regularly accept, it is traditionally associated with attempts to show that both sides have entered the freewill controversy under a misconception. For it is hard to deny that it is largely by a consideration of what a person could do if he wished, or tried, that we estimate his responsibility and the extent to which he is free. Hobbes defines a free agent as 'he that can do if he will or forbear if he will', Hume makes 'hypothetical liberty' the foundation of his 'reconciling project' of the *Enquiry*, and Mill claims that 'if we examine closely, we shall find that this feeling, of our being able to modify our own character *if we wish* is itself the feeling of moral freedom which we are conscious of'. Yet in spite of its good intentions and its honourable ancestry, such a move hardly withstands even the traditional comeback that real freedom is freedom of *choice*: if I can take an apple only if I choose to, and I cannot choose to, then I am not free to take the apple. Consequently, the objection continues, when moral responsibility is at issue, I must mean more by 'I could have moved my finger' than 'I could have moved it, if I had chosen to.' I must mean that I could have chosen, or 'willed', to move it.

[1] *v.* above, Ch. V, Pt 3, for a criticism of this argument.

This popular counter-argument, which commonly leads on to the curious wrangle about whether a man can choose to choose,[1] is really no more than a symptom of something wrong, since it entirely misses the real fallacy committed by Mill and his predecessors, which is that of taking 'I could, if I chose' as a genuinely conditional statement at all. *That* is why it is so plausible to say that by 'I can' I mean no more than that I can, if I choose. Not because the former, in spite of appearances, is, on 'close examination', recognisable as elliptical and really conditional, but because the latter, despite its form, is really categorical, a pseudo-conditional like 'It could light, if it were struck' or 'It is poisonous, if you drink it'; although, as we shall see, for not at all the same reasons.

How can this be shown? It might be enough to point out that the question whether a person chooses or wishes to do an action is irrelevant to the question whether he is able to do it, and that if all I need to do in order to get an apple is to choose to get it, then, quite categorically, I can get it. For it follows from this that 'I can, if I choose' is not really conditional. But it will pay us to suppose that our argument is addressed to someone who needs to be convinced on this very point.

As a first move, we can simply give examples. Just as we laboriously presented the contrast between 'The car could do 100 m.p.h., if there were a driver' and 'The car could do 100 m.p.h., if it were a Rolls', the former of which can reasonably be taken only as a pseudo-conditional, implying its own consequent, so we may bring out the same difference between, on the one hand, the genuine conditional 'He could reach it, if he were six inches taller' or ' . . . if it were six inches lower', and, on the other hand, 'He could reach it, if he tried' or ' . . . if he chose'. There is some variety here, since, for example, 'He could reach it, if it were needed', ' . . . if he were more helpful', ' . . . if he had the occasion' and even ' . . . if he knew it was there', are also pseudo-conditionals, raising special questions. For the present, however, we shall keep to one kind of example.

Language is actually less misleading here than in the case of natural power. There the issue was confused by the fact that sentences like 'It cannot light, unless it is struck', or 'It can only do 100 m.p.h., if

[1] *v.* G. E. Moore, op. cit., p. 135, and C. D. Broad, op. cit.

there is a driver', have an intelligible, idiomatic and fairly common use in which they express propositions regularly true of matches and motor-cars. 'He can only reach it, if he likes', or 'He cannot go, unless he wants to', do not have such a use. The special cases that may be constructed, e.g. 'You cannot come with me unless you really want to', prove the rule by their peculiarities. This point serves to emphasise the absurdity of an argument from the non-fulfilment of the quasi-antecedent to the non-fulfilment of the quasi-consequent, an absurdity utilised in a joke of Lewis Carroll's, which may be worth quoting in full:

'Well, how much have you learned, then?'
'I've learned a little tiny bit,' said Bruno, modestly, being evidently afraid of overstating his achievement. 'Can't learn no more!'
'Oh Bruno! You know you *can* if you like.'
"'Course I can, if I *like*,' the pale student replied; 'but I can't if I don't like!'
Sylvie had a way – which I could not too highly admire – of evading Bruno's logical perplexities by suddenly striking into a new line of thought; and this masterly stratagem she now adopted.[1]

Sylvie's reaction may be sadly unphilosophical, but to accept Bruno's argument would be to share the ludicrous position of a man who scraps his car because he has been convinced by the actualist that, because it is now motionless and motion demands an absent cause, it is not, strictly speaking, capable of taking him to work. Whatever is normally meant by 'He can, if he likes', the protasis is certainly not intended to refer to a necessary condition for the existence of the ability. Nor, of course, does it express a supposed sufficient condition. As Austin points out in this connection, from 'I can, if I choose to', we cannot deduce 'If I *cannot*, I do not choose to.'[2]

[1] *Sylvie and Bruno Concluded*. I am grateful to Renford Bambrough for pointing out this passage.
[2] 'Ifs and Cans.' As a matter of fact, such a deduction is allowable on one possible interpretation of, e.g., 'Smith can do it, if he tries to do it': i.e. on its interpretation as an 'inferential' conditional (*v.* above p. 81 f.) which would be true if Smith cautiously only ever tries to do what he can do. This is obviously no help to the theory of 'hypothetical liberty'.

Although Austin does not use it, there is also a general logical argument available which is sufficient to demonstrate that 'can' must not be construed as a 'can . . ., if . . .' taken to express a genuine conditional. Whatever we do mean by 'He can swim (here and now)' it seems at least clear that if someone swims, he can swim: *p* entails that *p is possible*. We do not also have to investigate the presence of a wish or the occurrence of a choice or effort, nor the 'voluntariness' of the swim, whatever exactly that is. But how could we know that any *conditional* is true simply from knowing that its consequent is true? *p* does not entail *if q, then p*, or *p, only if q*. We shall meet this negative principle again. Our intuitive readiness to agree that by 'he can' or 'he could' we mean 'he can, if he wishes' or 'he could, if he chose', tells us something about the latter rather than something about the former: namely, that the latter are not real conditionals.

Austin discusses another consideration that may mislead us into supposing that we are normally only prepared to ascribe powers conditionally. This is the fact that the commonest way of ascribing a power, in the past tense, is to use a 'subjunctive' or 'conditional' form of *can*, namely 'could have'. Hence we may readily think of 'He could have come' as an elliptical conditional statement, by analogy, presumably, with 'He would have come.' Austin himself thinks that this is a very important source of error. Nowell-Smith, whom Austin discusses, is an example of a writer consciously influenced by this factor. Austin is surely right to attribute to it a considerable unconscious influence. He argues that it rests on a grammatical mistake, and that it is wrong in these cases to classify 'He could have done *a*' as anything but indicative:

> To construe 'could have' as a past subjunctive or 'conditional' . . . is practically as much as to say that it needs a *conditional* clause with it . . . Once it is realised that 'could have' can be a past indicative, the general temptation to supply if-clauses with it vanishes.

Unfortunately Austin's argument seems to be itself mistaken. It *may* be correct grammar to argue that 'could have' is *never* subjunctive, since English has virtually no true subjunctive forms in living use, any more than it has a future tense, but mostly makes use of the past tense, auxiliaries and participles, where a subjunctive might be appropriate.

Yet if any 'could have done' is to be classified as a 'subjunctive' – and this Austin allows in the case of its occurrence in genuine conditionals – it seems that all must be. The thing to notice is simply that the subjunctive or 'conditional' mood does not only appear in conditional statements, any more than the optative in Greek appears only in the expression of wishes. In fact its function in the assertion of a possibility or ascription of a potentiality seems to be, in general, to 'hint' at the non-actualisation of the possibility (but not its non-existence) in the same sort of way as the use of the subjunctive in a conditional carries the implication (but does not logically entail) that the antecedent is unfulfilled. Consequently, so far as truth and falsity are concerned, there is no significant difference between 'You could have done it' and 'You could (were able to) do it', or between 'You can do it' and 'You could (would be able to) do it.' A shift of mood, or, more strictly speaking, a shift of tense in combination with the use of an auxiliary, may occur even when 'can' is not itself used: for example, from 'It was possible for you to come another way' to 'It would have been possible for you to come another way.' The important thing to realise is that such a shift does not necessarily make the ascription of the power in any way hypothetical. In this conclusion although not in his argument, Austin is absolutely correct. The importance of his philosophical discovery is not diminished by its obviousness now that it has been made. We need only add that his point has application to natural powers, as well as to personal powers.

At least two problems remain. Why is it that 'He could do it, if he tried' and similar pseudo-conditionals are not, as they evidently are not, real conditionals? Secondly, what is the function of the if-clause in these idiomatically irreproachable sentences, if it is not to make them conditional? It might be thought that the first question has been answered already, simply by the point that what a person wants to do is obviously not relevant to the question of what he *can* do.[1] But I now have to consider a theory that purports to offer a much fuller answer than this, and I shall be led to expand my own answer.

---

[1] The theme of a recently published book, *The Freedom of the Individual* by S. Hampshire. As Hampshire puts it, there is a 'line of distinction between *vouloir* and *pouvoir*'. Lack of will and lack of ability are explanations for the non-performance of an action that do not overlap. We need to understand why.

3. A REFUTATION OF THE ORTHODOX ACCOUNT OF 'I CAN', AS EQUIVALENT TO A CONDITIONAL STATEMENT

In my inquiry into pseudo-conditionals like 'This car could do 100, if there was someone to drive it', I reached an explanation of how it is that the subordinate clause fails to make the statement conditional, by an appeal to the distinction between intrinsic and extrinsic conditions, by drawing out the implications of the close relationship between a thing's potentialities and its intrinsic nature, and by an analysis that summarises the significance of this relation. This explanation added up to a refutation of actualism as it applies to natural powers, the view that things are capable only of what they actually do. The theory that I shall now consider attempts to do as much for pseudo-conditionals like 'He could, if he chose.'

I have mentioned the suggestions that 'He can tie reef-knots', 'He could run a mile' mean 'He ties reef-knots, if he tries' and 'He would run a mile, if he had a motive.' The doctrine that 'He could . . .' means 'He would . . ., if he chose' is obviously of the same general type. It is not surprising that such theories are popular, for they might seem to answer a number of problems with great economy, in an intellectually and even, as it is sometimes suggested, morally satisfactory way. The cursory exposition that follows may not do full justice to their plausibility. I shall not keep to the version of any one author.

The primary function which it is claimed that such a theory fulfils is that of avoiding the paradoxes of metaphysical determinism, the achievement of a reconciliation between scientific determinism and 'freewill', by explaining the distinction between personal power and its exercise; that is to say, by explaining how an unactualised possibility for choice is possible. The problem of what it can mean to say that a course of action is possible for an agent is explicitly represented as having been reduced to the general problem of conditional or dispositional statements, or, alas!, of 'counterfactuals'. C. L. Stevenson, in *Ethics and Language*, advances the theory in the form of a somewhat elaborate definition of an 'avoidable' action: ' "*A*'s action was avoidable" has the meaning of "If *A* had made a certain choice which in fact he did not make, his action would not have occurred." ' He then feels able to dismiss the problem of verification as one not specific to the topic of avoidability:

> When we say, 'if water contracted on freezing, ice would lie at the bottom of lakes', we do not deny that the actual behaviour of water is determined. Just as the contrary-to-fact condition in this statement about water does not imply indeterminism in physics, so the corresponding one in the statement about choice, included in the definition of 'avoidable', does not imply indeterminism in psychology.... The avoidability of a man's actions has nothing to do with the *causes* of his *actual* choice; it has to do with the *effects* that would have attended a *different* choice. (p. 299)

The second achievement that is commonly attributed to this theory is the explanation of why it is that '*ought* implies *can*', why it is logically inappropriate to enjoin or discourage, to praise or blame, or, for that matter, to reward or punish actions that are recognised as unavoidable. The purpose of moral judgements, it is said, is to alter or confirm, and generally to control, the behaviour of other people. This they achieve by building up attitudes in a man, by forming his 'character' perhaps, and thus determining his choice (ibid., p. 204). But since it is his actions that we are interested in, there is no point in determining an attitude or choice if this does not in turn determine an action. Hence it is only reasonable or useful to praise and blame actions that do depend on choice, i.e. that *would* have been otherwise *if* a different choice had been made, and if a different attitude had been present. That is why (it is said) we have the 'rule' that *ought* implies *can*, that blame presupposes avoidability.

The same argument can also be presented as an explanation of why we have the concepts that we do, of possibility, freedom and responsibility. It tries to explain these concepts in terms of their utility in directing sanctions against those whose behaviour sanctions are likely to affect. The theory is, of course, closely related to the classic utilitarian theory of punishment, and has been called the utilitarian theory of responsibility. It is also sometimes said to explain the conception of character. The moral character is defined as those dispositions that can be altered by moral exhortation. Intellectual dispositions like intelligence, on the other hand, cannot be so modified and therefore (it is said) do not form part of the character.

We might mention that exponents of this theory sometimes strike a note of self-congratulation, which suggests that it is a point in favour of their doctrine that it ties in with what they regard as the morally enlightened view that people ought to be held responsible and punished for bad actions that the punishment is likely to prevent in the future, and only for such actions. This suggestion can be discounted, for, as Hume remarks, no method of reasoning in philosophy is more to be condemned than that of trying to refute a hypothesis by a pretext of its consequences for morality. Of course, a philosophical theory, like a matter of fact, may have consequences for morality; which is one reason why it can be important to be right. But though we may think it right, for example, to treat all men as equal, the nobility of such conduct cannot make it more likely that all men are equal. The same point can be made against those who try to weaken the utilitarian theory of responsibility by making it appear morally repugnant.

Another possible attraction of the theory is that it seems to give some answer to a problem of meaning. If it is allowed that 'can', 'possible' and so on are not simply equivocal, that 'power' is not used homonymously when we talk of the powers of people and the powers of things, it might be thought that it must be possible to give essentially the same kind of analysis of 'He can . . .' as of 'It can . . .' An account of both as hypothetical or 'dispositional' statements might seem to fit the bill. It is true that we have discovered some striking differences between an acceptable account of natural power and the analyses of personal power most commonly offered. One form of the utilitarian theory, however, the suggestion that 'Smith could do a' is true when, and means that, moral exhortation, threats and so on would make Smith do a, does succeed in representing personal powers as very much like causal properties. Praise and blame, stick and carrot, play the part of stimuli such as we might apply to things in order to test their potentialities. This assimilation may seem a logically economical theory about the meaning of 'can', even if it must be admitted that other uses of 'can', for example, the *a priori* 'can', fail to fit into the same mould.

It hardly needs to be said that this type of analysis would explain in the simplest possible way why pseudo-conditionals like 'He could do it, if he tried', or 'You could do it, if you liked', are not to be taken as genuinely conditional assertions. It would be for exactly the same reason as 'It is fragile, if you drop it' would not normally be a real conditional. The explanation would extend to examples of pseudo-conditionals like 'He could do it, if he were honest', 'He can do it, if you ask him nicely', and even 'I could go, if there were an occasion to go'. In the last case, we might define an 'occasion' as a circumstance the presence of which influences choice, but the absence of which would not render the choice inoperative.

The utilitarian, 'stick and carrot' theory of responsibility can seem a promising piece of explanatory philosophy. Nevertheless a simple logical argument is enough to refute its basic tenet, and a brief inquiry will demonstrate the weakness of the rest of the structure.

No kind of possibility-statement can conceivably be analysed into hypotheticals like those suggested, simply because, as we have previously remarked, p entails that p *is possible*, whereas p does not entail that *if q, then p*. It was an essential aspect of our analysis of natural possibility and power that it involved only 'unspecific' hypotheticals. If something happens, that is enough to show that in some circumstances it happens, or that it does not necessarily not happen in any circumstances. For obvious reasons, it is never suggested that 'He could do it' is equivalent to the unspecific hypothetical 'In some circumstances, he would do it.' We are offered instead conditionals, or quasi-conditionals, with *specific* protases, '... if he wished', '... if he tried' and so on. As we shall see, there may be reason for denying that these locutions are genuine conditionals at all. But if we take them and the analysis at their face value, as intended, we have a clear counter-example to the theory in the case of someone who does something without trying, without wishing, or without choosing to do it. Such an action conclusively proves the existence of the ability, but could not be supposed to prove the correctness of a previous conditional assertion that the agent would do it if he tried, or wished, or chose to do it; just as the collapse of a bridge in a flood proves the possibility of its collapse, but not that it would have collapsed in a gale.

The view might be advanced that a man's performance of an action *is* by itself sufficient to verify 'He would do it, if he tried.' This may seem odd, but the concept of trying is a notoriously odd one. If Smith jumps seventeen feet without trying, it might be said, then, of course, he would have jumped it, if he had tried. That we say such things as 'You will not succeed unless you stop trying' is less an argument against this view than a demonstration of the slipperiness of 'try'. For has someone really stopped trying if he obeys the injunction to 'stop trying (to swing his arms loosely, to be happy) if he wants to succeed'? Stranger still, an effort might be required to 'stop trying'. We shall say more that relates to this 'slipperiness'. Yet if there is anything in this suggestion, it must surely make us examine more closely the pretensions of 'He would, if he tried' to be genuinely conditional, rather than doubt the validity of the principle that p does not entail *if q, then p.*

One kind of puzzle is likely to arise when we ask what it is to test this 'conditional', by comparison with testing something like 'If the fuse is lit, the charge will explode.' In the latter case we can see that, however indispensable some reference to parallels may be, the most direct kind of test would be to bring it about that the fuse is lit, and then observe the consequence. It might be held that, in just the same way, if we are to test 'He will, if he tries', we need to bring it about that the man tries to do the action in question (an end which we achieve, for example, by moral exhortation) and then we observe whether he succeeds, i.e. whether the action follows. Yet the proposition that he will do a particular thing if he tries to do it is surely, on the intended interpretation, one that the man himself can test; and there is not much sense in the notion that he must first do something, i.e. 'trying' to do the action, and then observe the result. The same thing might be said about 'He would . . ., if he chose' or '. . . if he wished'. Although a discussion of these might take a somewhat different course (compare doing something without trying to, with doing something without wanting to), I shall, for the sake of brevity, concentrate on *trying*, where the view we have to deal with is, if anything, most plausible.

It is often remarked that the analysis of an ordinary successful action, such as raising an arm, into two parts, the preaction of trying or willing to raise the arm (which is all that the agent really *does*) and the resultant 'action', is clumsy and unconvincing. One point is that there is difficulty in the concomitant notion that trying to do such an action is a means to the end of doing it. It may seem a truism that the only means of doing *any* action that one intends is to try to do it; but on the other hand this implies the vicious regress, that every action requires that another be done first, as means to it. And if some actions must be performed without the performance of another as means, as they obviously must be if any are performed at all, then the action of raising an arm is, in general, as good a candidate for this primary status as any.

One reason why it may look as if we have to do every intentional action by trying to do it will become clearer if we consider a characteristic example of someone doing something *without* trying to do it: for we find that it is not a man who has succeeded in doing an action without performing a normally prerequisite action, like making good tea without warming the pot, but simply a man who has done something unintentionally, by chance, by accident. The connection between trying and intending is obviously strong. 'Did you try to do that?' often means no more than 'Did you do that intentionally?' Of course, another kind of case of 'doing without trying' is that of an action done very easily; but here we are inclined to say 'almost without trying', as if we cannot quite bring ourselves to admit that an action done intentionally can be done entirely without trying, even if it is done without effort. But if it is insisted that every step I take intentionally must be accompanied by an act of trying to take it, we shall be hard put to it to find a referent for this description except for the times when walking is difficult, or when I am in doubt about my ability to walk, so that I step out tentatively. In fact, we might well wonder what, in normal circumstances, would conceivably count as trying or making the effort to take a pace, in order to fulfil the protasis of, and so to test, 'I would, if I tried'. It is easy to see that the concepts of choosing and wanting present similar, if not exactly parallel difficulties.

A related perplexity concerns the kind of connection 'He would . . ., if he tried (chose, wished, etc.)' is supposed to affirm between what we might call the protasis-fact and the apodosis-fact. It is a familiar point that species and particular cases of trying, wanting and choosing to do something are necessarily identified by a forward-looking reference to specific or particular acts, and, it often seems, by precious little else. Consequently the assertion that a causal relationship exists between trying to run and running, or between choosing to fly a kite and flying a kite, seems virtually vacuous by comparison with the claim that a naked flame in a room filled with coal-gas will produce an explosion. It is sometimes claimed, indeed, that only a logical relation can hold between an action and the respective choice, effort or desire.[1]

It is tempting to reply to this, that whenever someone tries to raise his arm and fails, then something, at any rate, happens – his arm twitches, his muscles bulge, his nerves are activated or at least his brain heaves: there need be no mystery about what 'trying' is if we identify it with such events as these. Yet if this argument shows anything, it is that we are concerned not so much with a queer event as with a queer concept. To take a quite simple case, a man trying to hit a target may be aiming straight at it when he pulls the trigger, and his *trying* may, let us grant for the sake of argument, consist in just this. But such an identification does nothing to explain the obvious logical difference, which is our present concern, between 'You will hit it, if you try' and 'You will hit it, if you aim straight at it and pull the trigger.' It is the former only, of course, that is supposed by philosophers to mean 'You can hit it.' The latter, very obviously, means nothing of the kind. In much the same way, an identification of 'trying to raise an arm' with certain unintentional muscular or nervous activity is irrelevant to philosophical difficulties about trying. For example, 'The best way to raise an arm is to activate such and such nerves' may be an odd kind of instruction, but on any interpretation it is not so completely vacuous as 'the best way, is to try'.

An attempt is sometimes made, particularly by the behaviouristically inclined, to explain trying not as, essentially, a means to the end of performing the action in question, nor as a feeling or act of effort accompanying the action, nor as a mental preliminary in any way causally related to the action, but simply as the part of the action that comes first (cf. Stevenson, op. cit., p. 301). Trying would then, presumably, be necessary to acting rather as running the first quarter of a mile is necessary to running a complete mile. Such a view may be made plausible by the thought that, if anything interrupts an action, preventing its completion, we are generally prepared to describe the agent as having tried to do it. The vacuity of the suggestion,

---

[1] E.g. A. I. Melden: *Free Action*; Charles Taylor: *The Explanation of Behaviour*. A classic debunking of 'volitions' as causes of actions occurs in Ryle's *Concept of Mind*, Ch. III.

that a good way to do an action is to try to do it, might also seem to be explained. But other aspects of the concept of trying are neglected. For example, no account is taken of the element of intentionality. We need to know why not everyone who runs a part of a mile is trying to run a mile. Moreover, the difference between 'You will run a mile if you try' and 'You will run a mile, if you run a quarter of a mile' is left entirely unexplained. Certainly the latter, or the former on any idiosyncratic interpretation that assimilates it to the latter, can hardly be supposed to be equivalent to 'You could run a mile.'

We shall return to this subject. It is not, however, necessary for the immediate argument to proceed to explore the concepts of trying, choosing, wishing, willing and the rest. It does not matter whether or not we are inclined to feel that there is anything to be said for assimilating 'He could' to 'He would, if he tried.' For everything that can be said for this view counts *against* construing the latter as a genuine conditional. As a matter of fact, 'He will do it, if he chooses to', '... decides to', '... wants to' are for various reasons much less plausible as equivalents for 'He can do it.' For example, if I try to do x, it at least seems that I am doing something appropriate towards testing 'I can do x' (which is not surprising, given the connection between 'try' and 'test'), but to want to do something, however passionately, is not yet to have done anything at all towards doing it or towards testing one's ability to do it. No doubt a sense of embarrassment at this fact has contributed to the philosophical, and chimerical, notion of a 'volition', a sort of executive wish, which, oddly enough, we perform. Yet however that may be, it does not affect the argument that personal power cannot possibly be explained by an analysis into genuine conditionals, as is envisaged in all varieties of the theory under criticism.

Objections might, however, be raised against the argument, and although they are somewhat involved, it might be as well to discuss them.

Firstly, it might be denied that p entails that *p is possible*, on some such ground as that one performance does not prove an ability, if it is a fluke. To this the reply can be made that, although one performance may not prove a general capacity, it could hardly be denied of a golfer who, however flukily, holed in one, that he was at that time able to hole in one. In any case, whatever else may be required in order to ascertain that a performance is not a fluke, the question certainly does not hang on whether the man is trying or wanting to bring it off. He may have been trying his hardest to hole in one, and yet his holing in one still be a fluke, although also a consequence of his trying. He presumably would not have holed in one, if he had not tried.

It might alternatively be held that, although 'He is doing *a*' does entail 'He can do *a*', the *former* cannot be established unless it is established that he was trying (or wishing, perhaps, or choosing or willing) to bring about the performance we observe: roughly, a real action must be 'willed', and an action is required to prove a capacity. And indeed, for whatever reason, something more than falling off a log may seem to be required, to prove the ability to fall off a log. Hence (it may be said) the fact that, in order to test a conditional, 'He will, if he tries', it would be necessary to establish that the protasis is fulfilled, does not prevent such a conditional from being equivalent to 'He can'.

This argument assumes the questionable analysis of every action into two elements. Nevertheless there is something about the peculiar relationships between trying, choosing, intending, wanting and the rest on the one hand, and *doing* on the other, that makes it plausible to say that acting without choosing to do so is not really acting,[1] that all doing is successful trying, or that all real actions involve volitions or desires to perform them. But such a view can hardly be supposed to help the argument for the 'utilitarian' analysis of avoidability. For both together would entail that all actions are avoidable. If 'He did it' entailed 'He tried (or willed, etc.) to do it', then it would be self-contradictory to assert 'Even if he had not tried (or willed) to do it, he would have done it.' This would be just like saying, 'Even if it had not broken, it would have broken into small pieces.' In that case it would also, of course, be self-contradictory to assert 'Even if he had chosen not to do it, he would have done it.' Yet this is just what Stevenson believes to be equivalent to 'His action was unavoidable.' Stevenson can hardly accept that the latter is self-contradictory, since it is claimed for his analysis that it explains the difference between avoidable and unavoidable actions, between those occasions when we do something because we have to do it, and other occasions when we do something although we could do otherwise.

[1] Cf., e.g., Nowell-Smith, op. cit., p. 278.

A third line of objection might claim that the principle that p never entails *if q, then p*, is false; consequently 'He will ... if he tries' might be entailed by its own consequent and be a perfectly respectable empirical conditional nonetheless. There is, of course, the view that *if p, then q* is always logically equivalent to $p \supset q$, but a more plausible argument might be backed by relevant-seeming instances. We mentioned an objection to treating 'He will, if he tries' as a genuine conditional, based on the *a priori* connection between trying to do an action and doing it. But this might be met by a comparison with, say, breaking and breaking into small pieces, or running in a particular race and winning it. 'If it breaks, it will break into small pieces', 'If he runs, he will win' are respectable (and non-truth functional) conditionals, in spite of the fact that it is at least as odd to talk of a causal connection between running in races and winning them as it would be, between choosing or trying to run and running. Moreover, it might look as if 'He will win' entails 'If he runs, he will win.'

Now these instances do demonstrate that the field of 'empirical conditionals' is a varied one, more so perhaps than our discussion so far has suggested. For example, we can test 'If it breaks, it will break into small pieces', but testing it would certainly not consist in bringing about one event and then observing whether another event occurs. A positive result, as well as a negative one, need involve the observation of one event only. Here p really does provide the most 'direct' confirmation of *if q, then p*. Nevertheless, these examples, in which the consequent implies the antecedent, will not support a case against my argument. For one thing, as we have just seen, if we are to analyse 'He could have done it' as 'He would have done it, if he had chosen to do it', we cannot suppose that 'He did it' entails 'He chose to do it.' We need to be able to say 'He would have done it, even if he had not chosen to do it.' Moreover, although a plate's breaking into small pieces is the most direct confirmation of 'If it breaks, it will break into small pieces', it is still not, by itself, conclusive confirmation, in the way in which someone's doing an action conclusively proves that he could do it. The other side of the same coin is that one observation, i.e. of the plate's breaking into pieces that are not small, would conclusively disprove the hypothetical, whereas one failure, not to speak of a wish or intention or decision not actually translated into action, does not prove the lack of a capacity. However eccentric the conditional proposed as an analogue to 'He will, if he tries', the essential difference between *if q, then p* and *p is possible* is not brought into doubt. As one school of philosophy might express it with effective exaggeration, the former is falsifiable but not verifiable, the latter is verifiable but not falsifiable. This is the very difference, of course, that has misled some philosophers into supposing that an analysis of 'can' as 'It's not the case that if . . ., then . . .' must always be possible (*v*. p. 110 of above). The utilitarian or dispositionalist theory of avoidability, which tries to obliterate this difference, so far from offering an account that preserves a unity of meaning for *can*, undermines the very principles that actually supply that unity. So far from reducing any problem about the verification of 'I can' to a general problem about hypotheticals 'counterfactuals' or dispositional predicates, the theory makes a mystery of its verification by denying the plainest truism. It certainly fails to lift us gently, as claimed, into the well-lit region of causality and law; plunging us instead into the territory of notoriously shadowy entities and baffling concepts, *choosing, trying, wanting, volition, motive* and the rest.

4. A CONTRADICTION IN DISPOSITIONALISM

The supporters of the utilitarian theory of responsibility are sometimes aware of some of the difficulties that we have discussed. Nowell-Smith, for example, explicitly excludes the concept of *trying* from his analysis, on the correct ground that the notion of a special act of trying would involve a vicious regress of tryings to try. He prefers to talk of 'motives', such as 'a passionate fondness for running', which he elsewhere describes as a disposition. Stevenson too, although he optimistically uses 'choice' ('by a convenient metonymy') to cover trying, willing, deciding, etc., all the 'manifestations of the will', and claims that the *nature* of choice is irrelevant to his analysis, nevertheless indicates that in his view choice should be thought of as a matter of attitude rather than as an act or introspectible event (op. cit., p. 305). Both writers, that is to say, seem prepared to think of the protasis of their analysans as itself in some way 'dispositional'. Such a view is perhaps found in its strongest form when Nowell-Smith comes to consider whether 'could have' sentences will submit to a conditional analysis 'in moral cases'. He remarks that some 'would ... ifs', for example, 'I would have kept my promise, if I had not been kidnapped', may excuse a man for failing to perform the consequent action, but others do not, e.g. 'I would have kept my promise, if I had been a more conscientious person.' His implication is that 'I *could* have kept my promise' can therefore be analysed as something like 'I would have kept my promise, if my character had been different.' And character is nothing if not disposition.

A theory of this kind may certainly seem to avoid the difficulty of identifying a sort of act, event or process that is to fulfil the role of 'trying', 'choosing' and the rest. It does nothing, of course, to escape the general criticism based on the principle that p entails that p *is possible* but does not entail that *if q, then p*. But the theory also has remarkable logical implications, remarkable because in violent conflict with the express aims of its proponents.

Nowell-Smith, for example, intends his 'if . . ., then . . .' analysis to prove that 'can' is 'dispositional'. Yet if the protasis of the analysans is itself dispositional, then, given his general presuppositions about dispositions and their relationship with hypotheticals, his theory would prove precisely the opposite. On his principles, the proposition expressed by 'If he were fond of running, he would run' must presumably be taken to have the same logical structure as the proposition expressed by 'If this were fragile, it would break.' The latter must in turn, presumably, be taken to be equivalent to something like 'If (if this were subjected to shock or strain, this would break), then this would break', which we can see is logically equivalent to something like 'This is being subjected to shock or strain', i.e. to something obviously not dispositional at all. Quite simply, the significance of asserting that $p = if\ q, then\ s$ is very much dependent on the value, and nature of q. If we accepted that *If (if p, then q), then q* is 'conditional', then any statement whatsoever could be shown to be logically equivalent to a conditional. If we also accepted that to be equivalent to a conditional is to be 'dispositional', then every statement is dispositional. Now, of course, a power, whether or not it is to be classified as a disposition, *is* a power, and 'He can do it' is therefore *not* like 'This is being dropped.' My point is that the orthodox analysis too evidently fails to explain the difference.

The issue can be presented in a slightly different way. Why is the orthodox analysis attractive? Surely because it seems axiomatic that a statement like 'John could either do it or not' is true when, and implies that, whether John does the action in question depends upon his 'will', that is to say, on his choice or preference. This dependence would then seem to be expressible by a hypothetical, 'If he prefers to do it, he will do it; if he prefers not to do it, he will not do it', which seems comparable to 'If the stone hits the water, there will be a splash; if it hits the bank, then there will not.' This hypothetical looks like an explanation of the expression 'It depends on his will' and so of 'He could either do it or not.' But is it so clear what *preference* is, as in 'He prefers walking to riding'? Why not argue that this means 'If he can either walk or ride, then he will walk'? It is at least as plausible to argue that 'he wants to' means 'he would, if he could' as that 'he could' means 'he would, if he wanted to'. It is clear that to advance both would be to complete a tight vicious circle.[1] The reasonable alternative is to regard both with suspicion. We might even rid ourselves of the prejudice that there are just two kinds of empirical statement, simple 'categorical' statements directly verifiable by observation, and hypothetical or 'dispositional' statements, a kind of complex of the former.

Exactly similar criticisms can be levelled against the attempt to explain power by bringing in the concept of moral character. We can hardly explain 'He could give £100 to the cause' as equivalent to something like 'If he were generous, he would give £100 to the cause', while at the same time explaining generosity as a disposition to perform such actions as giving money to worthy causes in appropriate circumstances. Again, it is surely more plausible to take 'John is generous' to mean something like 'John would give away money in appropriate circumstances, *if he could*', since a penniless man may still have a generous disposition, than to suppose that 'John could

[1] Cf. Austin, op. cit., pp. 174–5. Austin emphasises the formal invalidity of Nowell-Smith's argument, by the point that, from the premiss that p and q are together sufficient conditions for r (i.e. that *will* + *ability* = *action*) nothing can be concluded about q (ability) that could not equally be concluded about p (will). Nowell-Smith (op. cit., 2nd edition, footnote p. 290) grants this formal invalidity, but argues that there are nevertheless other reasons for his claim that q means *if p, then r*. But not only is his argument invalid, his position is self-contradictory.

give away money' means anything like 'He would, if he were generous'.

We may notice that here we have a reason for rejecting the orthodox view that statements about people's dispositions are analysable into hypotheticals about how they would behave in certain circumstances, how they would react to certain stimuli. 'Jack would knock Jill down, if she poked fun at him' no doubt normally lets us know that Jack is surly, sensitive and ungallant, or perhaps in a bad mood, but it also implies that he is capable of knocking Jill down. It suggests too something about his cognitive capacities, beliefs and so on – all of which counts against the possibility of disentangling anything like a Rylean, stimulus-reaction analysis of the meaning of 'surly' or 'sensitive'. It is a corollary that 'If John were irritable, he would knock James down' implies more than that John is in provoking circumstances, a point of contrast with 'If this were brittle, it would break' which in general goes unnoticed by dispositionalists. In fact it follows simply from the position that 'character' (or 'motive', or 'attitude' and so on) comprises a *third* variable knowledge of which, together with a knowledge of abilities and circumstances, will enable us to predict action – a position which, as we have seen, may actually form the basis of attempts to show that 'I can' is dispositional or hypothetical, and which, although vastly oversimple, is yet considerably different from the crude traditional conception of character elsewhere propounded by dispositionalists, embodied in the old deterministic formula, 'Same character, same circumstances, same act.'

5. FURTHER OBJECTIONS TO THE ORTHODOX VIEW

Whenever men notice some similarity between two things, they are wont to ascribe to each, even in those respects in which the two differ, what they have found to be true of the other.

Descartes

The analysis of 'I can' into hypotheticals gets much of its allure from its relation to a very general and *ipso facto* attractive philosophical attitude.

It is natural, and correct, to see a distinction between columns A and B:

A.	B.
This is red (hard, heavy, hot, bent, falling, etc.)	This is brittle (elastic, powerful inflammable, etc.)
	This can be bent (could fall, etc.)
He is in pain (thinking, swearing, running, raising an arm, reciting poetry, etc.)	He is irritable (intelligent, wicked, fond of running, capable of raising an arm, etc.)
	He understands French (knows *Hamlet* by heart, etc.)
He saved her	He could have saved her
The bough will break	If the bough breaks, the cradle will fall
	In some circumstances, the cradle would fall
etc.	etc.

We are concerned with the doctrine that this distinction can be explained by relating, or reducing, all members of column B to hypotheticals, which are seen as complexes of members of column A. What primarily offers itself as requiring such philosophical explanation is the 'unobservable' character of the states of affairs described by statements in column B. The division where I have made it is the most natural one, and I shall neglect the fact that some philosophers, for reasons perhaps special to each case, are able to find this unobservable character in thought, in pain, even in the colours of physical objects or the objects themselves.[1]

It should be clear by now that, if the term 'hypothetical' is applied to all statements of an 'If . . ., then . . .' grammatical form, then not all empirical hypotheticals deserve a place in column B. Our distinction is not one of grammatical form but of 'metaphysical' or semantic type. No grammatical form can guarantee semantic type.

---

[1] E.g., for Ryle, the mind 'is not the topic of sets of untestable categorical propositions, but the topic of sets of testable hypothetical and semi-hypothetical propositions'; for Locke, secondary qualities are 'mere powers'; for Mill, physical objects are 'possibilities of sensation'.

It is a central contention of this book that, while it may be useful and explanatory to relate some non-hypothetical members of column B to hypotheticals (for example, 'It could fall' to 'In some circumstances, it would fall'), any attempt to do so in other cases, in which the subject is a person, is mistaken in principle. I do not, of course, mean that it is mistaken *whenever* the subject is a person. For one thing, there is no reason why a person should not be brittle or inflammable. The case that particularly concerns us is that of the powers of people to do things.

The property that statements in column B possess in common is, of course, epistemological. Put crudely and incorrectly, it is that they can be known to be true or false only indirectly. Put more accurately, it is that reference to more than one occasion, to situations parallel to the situation in question (i.e. 'induction'), plays a necessary part either in the justification or in the refutation (or in both) of any member of the class.[1] An aspect of their epistemological peculiarity is that we especially think of them, or most of them, as verifiable by tests or trials. Why does this feature encourage the view that they can all be reduced to hypotheticals?

The two motives that we shall now discuss are both explicit in Ryle's *Concept of Mind*, a handbook of this kind of theory. The first is the view that all statements in column B (as well as, in Ryle's case, some of those in column A) perform a certain *function*: namely, that of 'inference-tickets', tools in the mechanics of the explanation, inference and prediction of (presumably) facts expressible by other kinds of statement (pp. 124–7, 142, 306). Since it is particularly easy to see how knowledge of the truth of a hypothetical like 'If babies need food, they cry' can help us to predict that Baby will cry or to explain why Baby is crying, it is easy too to conclude that all these supposedly 'explanatory-predictive' assertions are basically hypothetical.

Now this notion of the *function* of a type of statement or concept is a difficult one. Certainly our interest in acquiring any empirical knowledge may be in order to enable us to infer, explain or predict. Certainly a detective may be interested in the capacities of the suspect

---

[1] Perhaps more would need to be said in order to exclude some relational or quasi-relational statements, e.g. 'This clock is slow.' It is important that degree of relevance is ultimately a function of similarity, among other things.

(Could she have struck the blow left-handed?) in order that he may explain the crime, while the suspect may be eager to know the powers of the detective in order to predict whether she will get caught. But need it be said that 'He can do it' exclusively or even typically serves as a matrix of explanations and predictions? My desire to know my own powers is characteristically at its highest not when I am trying to predict or explain my actions, but simply when I am considering what to do. It might just as well be said that information about the powers of another performs its primary task when we are required to give him advice, seeing things from his point of view. The realm of possibilities – this kind of possibilities, at least – is essentially of interest when a choice has to be made, rather than when inferences need to be drawn. Perhaps little enough can be based on such a hazy conception of the primary 'context' or 'use' of a statement, but I would be quite content with this verdict if it is applied impartially. It is in any case pure philosophical prejudice to regard possibility as essentially an 'explanatory' concept.

An equally important misconception is the idea that if the characteristic method of verifying a statement is by conducting tests, then the statement must be equivalent to a hypothetical. Ryle appears to be strongly impelled by this notion, so closely does he couple the assertion that certain propositions are 'testable' with the assertion that they are hypothetical. (E.g. p. 46, quoted above, footnote p. 139; p. 25, p. 117 and, especially, p. 170.) Be that as it may, we can construct the sort of argument that must lie behind the view: to conduct a test it is necessary to set up certain conditions comprising a certain stimulus, and watch for certain results or reactions; hence, if the characteristic way of discovering the truth or falsity of some proposition is by conducting a test, then the proposition must be equivalent to a hypothetical proposition that in certain test conditions a certain result will occur.

It is too narrow a conception of what constitutes a test to think that testing can always be described in terms of stimulus and reaction, or as setting up conditions and observing consequences. Roughly, testing is just doing something, other than simply observing or getting into a position to observe, in order to verify a hypothesis. This is rough, for we *would* speak of testing the warmth of a bath with an elbow; but not of testing the colour of paint by going to look at it. When it is one of my own capacities that is in question, the relevant 'doing' that constitutes the test may simply be to exercise it. There is a great difference between a test for the presence of acid or hydrogen gas, and an intelligence test or driving test. Superficially, from one point of view, they may look the same sort of thing, the test-paper, the pen, the examination room and so on seeming to be on a par with the litmus paper or the lighted match. But if the litmus paper does not turn pink, then the liquid is not acid, whereas there is nothing, however generally or vaguely adumbrated, of which it can be said that if the subject placed in these circumstances, does not do, write, say or even think *this*, then he is not intelligent. The subject may, for example, be uninterested, unco-operative, not really trying, distracted or simply unable to read the language in which the test is written. It will not do to say that it is part of the test that these conditions should be avoided. They are not 'external' conditions, as we have previously noticed; but in any case I can test my own intelligence, and abilities in general, without having to bring about something called 'co-operation' or doing something called 'trying my best' and then observing the result. I simply set about some task that I know calls for powers of intelligence.[1] The model of the experiment in physics is inappropriate, and as this model becomes inadequate to explain what it is to test the truth of some proposition, so too the analysis of the proposition into a hypothetical becomes inappropriate, or particularly inappropriate.

If philosophical behaviourism constitutes a metaphysical failure to take one's own experience and thought seriously, the utilitarian theory of responsibility represents a similar failure to take seriously a man's relation to his own abilities and his special position when it comes to testing them. If we think always of testing the powers of *another* person, it is tempting to take it that the test of an ability essentially involves a process of getting him to do the action in question. Threats and promises, praise and blame admittedly can be ways of getting people to do things, and the utilitarian theory characteristically goes hand in hand with the popular doctrine that getting other people to do things is the 'function' of moral language that is somehow supposed to ex-

[1] Of course, it may not be easy to choose a specific task, the performance of which will give the right kind of very general information about my capacities. Intelligence tests are difficult to devise.

plain its meaning. Given this queer enough doctrine, together with an equally odd and unjustified preparedness to find a special 'sense' of *can* tailor-made for 'moral discourse', we arrive at the conclusion that it is the meaning of 'Smith could have done it' that appropriately directed praise and blame, threats and promises, would have got Smith to do it, and that to ask whether an action is free is to ask whether it is the sort of action to be influenced by methods of persuasion. To help us to achieve a philosophical understanding of the question 'Could So and So have done such and such?' we are given the picture of an ideal moralist or judge investigating the dispositions and capacities of other men, in the same way as a physicist or chemist investigates the dispositional properties and powers of substances. The moralist's interest is allowed to be practical, but only in the way in which the physicist's too may be practical if he has an eye to controlling and manipulating, as well as understanding, what is before him. The legislator is encouraged to use his crude stimuli, approbation and rebuke stick and carrot, like a schoolboy scientist wielding his sulphuric acid and glowing splints; and he is given *a priori* the queer assurance that failure in achieving his ends will reflect the incapacities of his human material.[1]

We are not now concerned with the question whether a complacent acceptance of this theory indicates a tolerable attitude towards one's fellow men, but with its intellectual shortcomings. Remind ourselves that we ourselves are men capable of action, and these shortcomings become obvious. The theory owes its plausibility to the concentration of attention on the context of praising and blaming others, or, more precisely, of encouragement and discouragement, to the exclusion of the context of deliberation, which is what gives the ground for the traditional description of moral questions as practical questions, and in which we are interested in our own capacities. For it surely does seem ridiculous to suppose that my knowledge that I could now go for a walk if I wished is knowledge that I could be induced to go for a walk

---

[1] For this central contention of the utilitarian theory, *v.* especially, Schlick: *Problems of Ethics*, Ch. VII; Stevenson, op. cit., pp. 301–18; Nowell-Smith, op. cit., pp. 300–6; Ebersole: 'Free-choice and the Demands of Morals', *Mind*, 1952, pp. 248–54. Cf. Hume: *Treatise*, pp. 608–9.

The doctrine is roundly condemned by Mabbott: 'Freewill and Punishment', *Contemporary British Philosophy*, 3rd Series, ed. Lewis.

by some moral argument or another. When, before facing a decision whether or not to do an action, I consider whether I can do it in these circumstances, I am surely not considering whether praise and blame would be likely to lead me to do it, nor asking myself the question whether somebody else could persuade me to do it. Why should I be interested in such a question? Yet when somebody else later comes to ask about me, perhaps in a law-court, whether I could have done the action, he will be asking just the same question as I am now asking, as it very well might be, in a 'moral' context. If he knows that I could have raised my arm at this moment, he will know what I now know, something that is certainly true and that I am now in the best conceivable position to test and to prove conclusively by action, whether or not I choose to do so. His knowledge, like my knowledge, is just obviously not some more or less recondite sociological information about arm-raising and its correlation with the sanctions of society.

6. THE VERIFICATION OF 'I CAN': MORE ABOUT TRYING

It is a platitude that we learn what we can do by trying. It will help us to understand the verification of propositions about what people can do, if we consider once again the concept of trying. But it will help us to understand the concept of trying if we see that it is, logically as etymologically, very closely related to that of testing. What is tested is, of course, an ability. We are concerned, therefore, with correlative terms. Consequently anyone who imagines that an analysis of ability in terms of trying is a simplification of what is complex, is chasing his own tail.

It is about as sensible to think of trying as itself a peculiar inner activity over and above the doing of the action, as it would be to think that testing the causal powers of a substance is a further activity transcending the action of, say, heating it. But there are significant differences between the cases. If I want to know whether I can hop on one leg, I try. Hopping about on one leg *is* trying when, as it happens, my trial gives a positive answer. If I fail, on the other hand, and simply totter about, then my abortive performance is my trying. That both the action and the abortive action are cases of trying to (i.e. of seeing if I can) hop about, does not imply that there is some further activity, whether 'inner' or neurological, in common to both performances; but simply that both performances have the same point. Now the situation is different when two ways of testing a substance for the same property have nothing in common but their point; for example, as we see whether something is explosive both by heating it and by dropping it. For in this case both heat and shock are seen by the experimenter as appropriate methods of causing an explosion if the substance is explosive, whereas I do not see tottering about or falling over, which may be all that I do when I try to hop on one leg, as appropriate ways of hopping on one leg if I can. My tottering can be said to have the same point as successful hopping, because it is a manifestation of my intention to hop if I can: but it is not intended to bring about my hopping since it is not intended at all. I may be doing nothing that I intend. It is in virtue of being the manifestation of an intention that an abortive action is *trying*. It is a mistake to think that no event can be identified as *trying* unless it is an intentional action. It need not even be capable of being seen as a way of getting the action done, nor as a part of the action, nor as a part of the causal chain issuing in action. Here is the difference from testing a physical substance: for we have not carried out a test on a substance unless we have done something to it that is capable of being seen as a means to producing a relevant reaction, and as a cause of that reaction.

We have already mentioned the necessary truth that not every action requires another as means to performing it: not every action has to be, or could be, 'brought about', some must simply be done. It is a related truism, which is among the data on which any reasonable theory about personal power must be based, that the experiment or trial verifying the existence of an ability may simply be the action in question. Trials need not always have some element of action in common independent of their result in the way in which a successful and an unsuccessful attempt at hitting a golf ball may sometimes have in common an identical swing. Thus the possibility of any hypothetical analysis of personal power is ruled out. In fact, that testing one's ability to do something is not the same kind of thing as testing the truth of a hypothetical, simply follows from the truism that in order to do something it is not always necessary to do something else first.

The temptation to think of *trying* as such a preliminary element of action, whether transcendental or neurological, is doubtless increased by the fact that the concept of trying is not tied as closely as is that of testing to an epistemic context. That is to say, the purpose of trying to hop on one leg may well not be to find out anything at all, but simply, say, to create a topic of conversation, or to obey a command. It is not difficult to understand how basically epistemic terms like 'try', 'attempt', 'essay' can find a place in other contexts. It is, for example, natural that such expressions should be used when success is in doubt: to say 'I'll try' may not imply a primary interest in the acquisition of knowledge or in the proof of a hypothesis, but it does imply a lack of certainty. It is also natural to apply the expression 'trying to walk' to all cases of failing to walk, irrespective of the agent's reason for walking. For something is learnt, although it may be incidentally. In a similar way we sometimes extend the notion of a test so far as to say that a car was tested by a rough road, even when the journey was not undertaken as an experiment. The difference is that it is easy to be led by the frequency of the non-epistemic use of 'try' to think of it as central or normal; which is dangerous because such cases are relatively unrevealing.

It is, of course, part of the basic concept of a trial, as of a test, not only that something is learnt but that something is intended. And it is perhaps the latter element that contributes most to the currently wide use of 'try', so that 'Were you trying to do that?' means simply 'Did you do that intentionally?', something very different from 'Were you seeing whether you could do that?' But I shall not now attempt to explore fully the source of the fallacious model that depicts trying as itself an activity that we perform in order to produce actions, or as an event that occurs with the effect that the intended actions are produced. My present aim is simply to say something in explanation of the relation between trying to do an action and being able to do it, a relation that is commonly and importantly misunderstood in philosophical theories about the nature of ability.

If I do *not* now try to raise my arm, or try to count up to a hundred, how do I know that I can now do these things? The answer is platitudinous – by induction. I have done them in circumstances not materially different from the present, and have not failed in doing them except when things were materially different. If someone wished to cast doubt on my belief, then he would have to point to something in the present circumstances (which include my own present state) *and* provide evidence that it represents a material difference from those past occasions, an obstacle that was then absent. His own argument, that is to say, must be inductive too, for he must provide evidence that I or people like me have tried and failed in the presence of this factor or set of factors. If I now successfully perform the action, he is normally refuted and must admit either that the factor is absent after all or that it is not as significant as he thought; although conceivably he might say that there has been a quick change in the situation between his claim and my trial. In the last case, once again, for his claim to be confirmed, the change would have to be identified and shown to be significant by reference to other trials. Moreover, to try and to succeed, i.e. to perform the action successfully, is to prove conclusively that one can do the action, but a failure, or the abandonment of an attempt, does not prove as conclusively that one cannot, or could not. However often I try and fail, it is conceivable that more effort, or perhaps some avenue that I have not yet tried, would lead to success. There is always the logical possibility that what seems impossible is only very difficult.

There is an even more obvious but philosophically extremely important asymmetry between the evidence for and the evidence against 'I can'. Any performance of the action in question, intentional or not, is potentially confirmatory evidence. But not any non-performance is relevant evidence against. The form of the argument 'You went for a walk yesterday (today is like yesterday) so you could go today' is acceptable in the way in which 'You did not go for a walk yesterday, so you cannot go today' is not acceptable. The non-performance must be a positive failure, i.e. at least a case of trying to perform, if it is even to be relevant. With this goes a limitation on the kind of factor in the situation which can be relevant, and this is the limitation commonly overlooked by determinists. For example, the queer argument that although I went for a walk yesterday I cannot go today because today I do not want to go, presupposes that the absence of a wish is a kind of factor that determines ability; i.e. that it is an obstacle. To support this presupposition it would be necessary to give instances of people lacking the wish to go for a walk or the like, who nevertheless tried to go for a walk, and failed because of the absence of the wish. Perhaps some sense can be made of this description, but, if so, it could only apply, on a special interpretation, to outlandish, quasi-pathological cases: only in such cases could the absence of a 'wish' be regarded as a factor limiting a power. Similarly an appeal simply to the non-performance of certain lazy people like myself would not support the claim that I cannot go for a walk, if the people in question had not tried to walk. For in that case their ability was not put to the test, and so their cases are irrelevant. Exactly the same goes for psychological powers. If someone never tries to concentrate on one thing for a long time, then the fact that he never does think in a concentrated way does nothing in itself to show that he, or anybody else who is like him, is incapable of mental concentration.

The epistemological relationship between trials and abilities can explain, then, why what a person chooses or wants to do, or what kind of person he is morally, or whether or not he had a motive or occasion for doing something, are all irrelevant to the question of what he *can* do. The complex and ultimately implausible superstructure of the utilitarian theory of responsibility, or of any other hypotheticist theory, is unnecessary for the task. It is therefore unnecessary as an explanation why such pseudo-conditionals as 'He could, if he wished' are not genuinely conditional, or as an explanation of the distinction between personal power and its exercise.

A discussion of the inductive verification of ascriptions of unexercised powers is an appropriate context in which to mention briefly another kind of theory about the meaning of 'I can'. In determining inductively whether a man could run we should naturally have to inspect the condition of his limbs and muscles. For we know from experience that muscles are important. This may lead to the view that 'Smith can run' is a kind of short-hand description of Smith's observable state. On one account, it is a negative description: it means, for example, among other things, 'Smith's leg muscles are not damaged.' A more sophisticated version of the theory, however, avoids a crude identification of the meaning of a possibility-statement with any such description, but asserts instead that the concept of ability is 'defeasible'. By this it is meant that directions for the use of the concept cannot be given as a list of necessary and sufficient conditions, but only by an open-ended list of negative conditions. 'He could run (if he wanted to)' is supposed to be explained by something like, 'He is *not* injured, or exhausted, or tied up, or drugged, and so on.' As one writer expresses it, 'we can accept certain evidence as evidence that [freedom] is absent, but there can be no evidence that it is present in a given case.'[1]

One objection to this kind of explanation – and there are others – is that obstacles are seen as obstacles just because it is known from experience that they limit the ability in question. To try to explain the notion of ability by means of such a list of obstacles or excuses is to put the cart before the horse. Yet the theory enjoys some acceptance, not only because of a traditional, circular effort to solve the freewill problem by explaining freedom as absence of constraint,[2] but also because of the supposed significance of the legal procedure for determining responsibility, under which responsibility for a past action is assumed unless the defence can make out a case that special circumstances obtained. We shall see that the question of a man's *responsibility*, and that of his *freedom*, are significantly distinct from the question whether 'he could have acted otherwise'. Moreover, legal 'defeasibility' reflects, not some mysterious logical distinction between positive and negative properties, but a particular answer to the practical question of where the burden of proof ought to lie. For our present purposes, the most important point is that concentration on the kind of example that normally comes before the lawcourts, when the situation in question is relatively long past, is liable positively to exaggerate the importance of induction in answering a question about ability, and so the importance of the observable conditions of each case. We should not allow the peculiarities of legal procedure to prevent us from thinking of a wider range of more everyday examples. It can hardly be supposed that my belief that I could now raise my hand might be expressed more simply as a belief in the absence of some set of

---

[1] J. D. Mabbott, op. cit. The chief authority for this kind of view (of which I have presented a much simplified version) is H. L. A. Hart: 'The Ascription of Responsibility and Rights'; but cf. also Austin: 'A Plea for Excuses'.

[2] v., e.g., Hume: *Treatise*, Bk II, Pt III, sect. II; Ayer: *Philosophical Essays*, Ch. 12.

conditions. For I can verify my belief directly without concerning myself with my observable state or situation. I can learn by trial that I have or that I lack the power of raising my hand, without knowing just why I have it, or lack it.

8

Deliberation, Freedom and Meaning

1. INTRODUCTORY

I have now offered explanations of the three main types of possibility that I set out to explain, and have tried to demonstrate that many philosophers, both determinists and indeterminists, but not only determinists and indeterminists, have misunderstood them and the relations between them. In this final chapter I shall try to round out my argument in three different but not entirely separable areas. First, I shall examine more closely the nature of questions involved in deliberation, then I shall consider how possibility for choice is related to responsibility and 'freedom' and, last, I shall make some remarks about the meaning of words like 'possible' and 'can'. These large questions will necessarily be dealt with very briefly.

2. MORE ABOUT POSSIBILITY AND THE CONTEXT OF DELIBERATION; AND ABOUT THE RELATION BETWEEN POWER AND WILL

The distinction between power and act is nowhere more obvious than in the context of deliberation, since it is the same as the distinction between the questions 'What can I do?' and 'What shall I do?', the first of which calls for a judgement about the situation, while the latter calls for a decision to act, or for advice. Paying attention to these questions can help us to understand possibility for choice.

It is not a new point that the relationship between these questions can give us an understanding of why '*ought* implies *can*'; which is one of the things that the 'utilitarian' theory of possibility purported to explain. In order to represent this relationship, we might imagine a sort of ideal deliberation, in which the question of what can or could be done is carefully settled before the question of what to do is attacked; but this picture should not be taken too seriously. There is as a rule an indefinite number of courses of action open to us that we do not even bother to consider as possibilities, whether because they are not in any case what we would want to do, or because the variations between them are unimportant. I do not wonder, every time I pass a bank, whether I could successfully rob it, and then, if I think it possible, consider whether or not to do so. The range of possibilities that we actually envisage is limited by our purposes and, perhaps, our moral principles, as, in turn, our aims are limited by our conception of what is possible. But it is not logically inappropriate to consider whether one could do an action, knowing that one would not choose to do it anyway, as it would be inappropriate to consider whether to do an action, after recognising that it is beyond one's power anyway. To be intelligible, the question must be whether one would do it, if one could. All this is platitudinous, but it explains the source of the principle that 'ought implies can'. For the question 'What ought I to do?' obviously only arises when the question 'What shall I do?' can arise: i.e. when more than one possibility is open.

Now the utilitarian would have to give a very odd explanation for the relationship between 'Shall I do it?' and 'Can I do it?' Presumably he would have to say that in deliberating what to do I am trying to influence myself to act, by exposing myself to practical or moral arguments. He must argue that it is pointless to bring pressure to bear on myself when this pressure will not have the desired effect. Therefore, before I deliberate whether to do an action, it is a good idea to determine that I *can* do it: that is, on the utilitarian analysis, that moral argument will get me to do it.

But it is absurd to represent deliberation as a procedure of trying to influence oneself in a particular direction, since if someone knows in which direction he wants to influence himself, his deliberation is already done. Nor is deliberation a process of trying to bring oneself to perform *some* act successfully, no matter what. The end of deliberation is not to screw oneself up to the point of acting, but to determine rationally which course of action to follow. In any case, the relationship between 'Can I?' and 'Shall I?', is surely at least as intelligible in itself as the related principle by which the utilitarian purports to explain it: that it is unreasonable to adopt a means (moral exhortation) to a desired end (some action on the part of oneself or another), when it is known that the means will not achieve the end. Moreover, the principle that *ought* implies *can* does not simply reflect a desire on our part not to waste breath or inner monologue. There is a real unintelligibility in 'Although you cannot do it, you ought to do it', the same as there is in 'Although I cannot do it, I intend to do it.' There is not the same unintelligibility in 'I gave him good advice, although I knew he would not take it' or in 'I know this will make no difference, but you ought to give yourself up.'

A consideration of what it is to decide can help us further towards an understanding of the relationship between capacity and 'will'. I have already approached this question from other points of view: I have discussed pseudo-conditionals like 'He could . . ., if he wished', and I have given an account of the verification of 'I can' and the nature of trying. I have argued that there is something unintelligible about the supposition that certain factors, desire, effort, occasion, motive, character and so on might determine what a man could do. This is borne out by the paradox involved in the supposition that someone might be attacking the question 'What can I do?' by asking whether a proposed course of action is sufficiently characteristic of him, whether he is honest enough to be *able* to hand in the lost property, or sufficiently motivated by generosity to be *capable* of giving five shillings to charity, or rash enough or bored enough to have the *power* to accept the strangers' invitation to play cards. We should have to say that he is considering, in somewhat indirect and misleading language, not the question 'What can I do?', but the question 'What shall I do?'; that he is considering reasons, not obstacles; and that he is making up his mind, not determining whether there is any need to come to a decision. The determinist and indeterminist both commonly misrepresent questions about a person's character or motives as being of the utmost relevance to the question of what he can do, and suggest that if we commonly neglect these questions about ourselves in determining what it is possible for us to do, we do so through ignorance and under an illusion. On the contrary, to pay any regard to them at all would be to change the character of the question, or, which is the same thing, to do what is logically inappropriate to the question actually asked.

Most determinists try to allow a place for deliberating what to do by the argument that, although our actions are determined by motives, character and the like, and so we could not act differently, yet our deliberations, reasonings and decisions form part of this causal process and therefore make a difference. Hence, they allege, it is not correct to infer from determinism the fatalist conclusion that deliberation has no point. But this attempt to save appearances is a mistake, in conflict with the obvious truth from which the fatalist starts, that if I know that there is only one thing I can do, even if I do not know what this is, it is not only pointless but logically absurd to set about determining an answer to 'What shall I do?' by weighing up reasons for courses of action.[1] For this is like saying 'There is only one thing I can do, but I have not yet decided whether to do it.' If a man can only do one thing, it follows that his 'decisions' are ineffectual. The best moral to draw from this, however, is not that we should fatalistically do and decide nothing, but that it is mistaken to suppose that motives determine ability to act. Our deliberations make a difference to what we do, but not to what we can do. But if one must be a determinist, it is better to be a fatalist.

Once again our thesis can be contrasted with a 'utilitarian' analysis of possibility for choice. That account may recognise that we do not allow a person's character to be relevant to the question of what he can do, but represents this assumption of irrelevance as somehow arbitrary: as though we arbitrarily make a distinction between 'causes' in refusing to take character into consideration, yet are not engaged on an essentially different kind of question because of it. This is actually the considered view of Nowell-Smith. 'He could have acted otherwise', he says, is 'thought to be' a necessary condition of 'He broke a law or moral rule', 'He deserves censure (or punishment)' and 'It would be just to censure (or punish) him', 'only because we exclude those cases of incapacity to act otherwise in which the incapacity lies in the moral character. If it is due to an external force or to a "compulsion" (which we talk of as if it were an external force), or to some non-moral defect,

---

[1] Cf. R. Taylor: *Metaphysics*, Ch. 5. An interesting recent exposition of fatalism, which correctly attacks what its author calls 'soft determinism'.

the incapacity to act otherwise is allowed to excuse; but not if it is due to a moral defect' (*Ethics*, p. 301). It is my contention, however, that it is logically impossible for an incapacity to 'lie in the moral character', and that this impossibility reflects, not some arbitrary distinction between moral and non-moral defects adopted for utilitarian reasons, but a fundamental and inescapable categorical and epistemological difference.

A man's character is logically unlike his capacities. It is related to them neither by determining them nor by being determined by them, but rather by being a 'logical construction' out of what a man does when he could act differently. That is to say, it is only because we can identify a class of actions as instances of choice between possibilities that we can have a conception of the character as something knowable or as something that explains behaviour. Knowledge of real ability is logically prior, not, as Nowell-Smith implies, posterior to knowledge of the character. Moreover, to understand the nature of the explanation of a man's actions that can be achieved by reference to his character, it would be necessary to trace very fully its relationship with explanation in terms of motive; for to explain a man's action as springing from his character as, say, a jealous or an honest man, is at least to impute certain motives, that is, reasons and intentions. The classification of underlying dispositions or character traits is therefore posterior to the conception of an action done for a reason; and reasons are always reasons for choice between possibilities. The common conception of character as something necessitating action is incoherent. There is only a trivial way in which an incapacity could be due to a moral defect, e.g. if a man drinks himself incapable.

Here we should issue another warning against the misleading character of 'ordinary language'. For we might very well describe an honest man as incapable of theft, or assert that it is not possible that such a man should tell a lie. We might mean by this simply that it is certain that he does not steal or lie, or else we mean that he would not steal or lie in any circumstances. But we do not mean that it is literally beyond his power to utter a falsehood, any more than we suppose that the secretary whom we praise for her accuracy in spelling is literally 'incapable of misspelling a word'. To say of someone that he is incapable of doing the decent thing is normally to criticise rather than to excuse. An appeal to cases in which he has tried his hardest and yet failed would go to refute, rather than to support, the point intended.

The mistaken idea that a man's powers are limited by his character also gets some strength from the fact that the agent under compulsion provides a natural model, but only a model, for talking about all kinds of reasoning. We often say that someone who follows a train of reasoning to its conclusion is 'compelled' to accept the conclusion. This tendency is probably at its strongest when the argument is deductive, but the same sort of model is applied to practical reasoning, when the conclusion is a decision to act, or advice. When I say that honesty compels me to do something, I may mean simply that my action is 'compelled' by considerations of honesty, rather than that it is a manifestation of an honest disposition. Thus the modest man may seem to shrug off responsibility for some praiseworthy action, with 'It was the only possible thing to do – it would have been wrong to do otherwise.' We do not take him seriously, since the wrongness of an action is no real obstacle to doing it. If a man recognises that a course of action is literally impossible, he cannot be said to reject it for a reason such as 'because it would be dishonest' or 'because it would cause hardship'. He does not reject it at all, since in recognising its impossibility he sets it aside, apart from those courses of action that are to be rejected or chosen. We should not be misled by the picture of decision what to do as the narrowing down of the field to the one 'possible' course of action, into accepting the thesis of determinism that everything else is beyond the agent's power.

A familiar kind of example is that of the prisoner forced at pistol-point to sign a false confession, of whom we might say that there is only one course of action open to him. Yet he adopts this course for a reason, 'because otherwise I shall be shot'. According to a traditional way of looking at such a case, the man with a gun provides an insuperable motive, say, fear, and this motive is what compels the prisoner to sign.[1] Hence we do not blame him. It is true that the sight of a gun might just put someone in such a panic that he loses control of his actions. Yet all that need happen is that, of the two genuinely open possibilities of signing or accepting the consequences, he accepts the

---

[1] Cf. Hume: *Treatise*, pp. 312–14.

one that seems more reasonable. If we do not blame him, it may simply be because it seems more reasonable to us too, not because we deem it literally out of his power to do anything else. He is indeed compelled, but by a man with a gun who really does limit the possibilities, not by the 'motive', which acts within the possibilities. It is philosophically unfortunate that we can express the fact that only one possibility is reasonable, by saying 'It is the only thing he can do', or even 'He has no choice.'

The difference between real compulsion and being 'compelled' by reasons can be brought out by an analogy from games-playing. In a game like chess, we often want to say that a player is compelled to do something, that he has only one possible move. Sometimes this is because of the situation together with rules of the game, for example, when it is necessary to move a King out of check. But sometimes we might say that a player is compelled to retreat his Queen, when the rules leave other possibilities open. The former is an analogue for real unavoidability, although only an analogue, since it may always be possible, for example, to overturn the pieces. The latter is a case of acting for a reason. It would be a mistake to argue that in this case, since the player is not compelled by the rules, he must be compelled by a motive, his desire to retain his Queen or his eagerness to win. It would be a mistake because our metaphor of compulsion has its springs, not in the strength of the 'desires' of the player, but in the strength of the reasons, within the game, for making a particular move. There would be little inclination to say of a player who deliberately left his Queen in danger, that he was compelled by his desire to lose. Of course, we cannot then say that he was compelled to retreat it, but the metaphor of compulsion ceases to be appropriate, not because the reasons lose their force, but simply because the action was not performed. His action is like that of a prisoner who chooses to be shot rather than sign a confession: he refuses to do the 'only possible' thing. It is tempting to suppose that the difference between the prisoner who reluctantly signs and the prisoner who, in the same situation, chooses to be shot, must be explained by a difference in capacity, in powers of resistance or 'will-power'. But strength of will and obstinacy are not so much capacities as traits of character; and in any case the difference may simply lie in a difference of values. The 'impossible' move, the impossible' choice are like the impossible candidate: as the dictionary puts it, 'not tolerable or reasonable'.

Yet probably by much the most powerful force operating towards a denial of any significant role for 'What shall I do?' once 'What can I do?' has been answered, is a set of arguments based on the confusion between possibility for choice and natural possibility, or at least on a misconception of the relation between them. We allowed that something may be implied about a man's character by the proposition that it is impossible that he should perform a certain kind of action, which is like the proposition that in no circumstances would he do it, and so seems closely comparable to the attribution of a natural power. (There is some reason for denying that the comparison is all that close: e.g. there is a possible distinction between 'He would not do it in any circumstances' and 'He would not do it *voluntarily*, in any circumstances.' Normally the latter is meant, of course.) Now it may be argued that, whatever may be said about any subtle distinctions between natural possibility and possibility for choice, one aspect of their relationship is clear: if something is within my power to choose, then it must be naturally possible too. It cannot be within my power to choose to turn lead into gold, or to jump thirty feet, if it is a natural impossibility that lead should become gold or that a man of my physique should jump thirty feet. It seems, then, that what it is impossible *that* a person should do is also impossible *for* him to do; and that, therefore, character does determine ability.

A more complex variant of the same argument brings in the notion of a 'necessary condition'. If A is a necessary condition for B, then in order to bring about B, I must first bring about A. If possession of a jemmy or of explosives is a necessary condition for robbing a bank, and I have neither a jemmy nor explosives, and can get neither, then I cannot rob a bank. Whatever 'I can' may mean, that much is certain. I cannot do any action a unless any necessary condition for its performance is fulfilled or can be fulfilled. If such a necessary condition, call it NC^1, is itself dependent on a necessary condition, NC^2, then I cannot do a unless NC^2 is fulfilled or, in turn, can be fulfilled. Admittedly, however long the chain of unfulfilled necessary conditions, if I can perform the first, NC^n, the action a is not prevented. But there is one situation in which I certainly could not fulfil NC^n, even if NC^n is not something naturally impossible in itself. This is when NC^n is an unfulfilled condition that must *have been* fulfilled if I am to do the action: for example, it may be a necessary condition for my getting lunch for a guest today, that I should have signed a list yesterday. If I have not signed the list, nothing impossible in itself, then I cannot get lunch.

Now according to scientific determinism, so the argument may proceed, events, including actions, do not just happen or fail to happen. If an event is not going to occur, this will be because some necessary condition, NC^1, is not fulfilled. NC^1 may, of course, be a set of factors, or it may require a disjunctive proposition to state it. If NC^1 is not fulfilled, this, in turn, will be because of the non-fulfilment of NC^2, and so on, by an unbroken regression to the present and indeed into the past, so that we can say that the event will not occur because NC^n is not now fulfilled, and because NC^{n+1} has not been fulfilled in the past. If it is a necessary condition for my robbing a bank in the immediate future that I should possess a jemmy and bear a grudge against society, and if it is a necessary condition for this anti-social attitude that I should have had such and such an upbringing, and if I did not have this upbringing, then a reason why I am not going to rob the bank, is because a *past* necessary condition has not been fulfilled. It follows (the determinist will claim) that I cannot rob the bank – for I cannot do any action if some necessary condition for doing it that must have been fulfilled, has not been fulfilled. And so for every action.

All variants of this argument[1] commit the same kind of mistake. This is contained in the simple appeal to the principle that if anything is possible for choice, it must be naturally possible. The field over which this principle can be applied is much narrower than the determinist imagines. Its limits are set by the paradigm impossibility of turning lead into gold, for the principle is correct when the 'anything' is some event that may be thought of as being *brought about* by what someone does. That is to say, the cash value of the principle is the platitude that I cannot bend a stick that is not pliable and, in general, no one can bring about a change c in a thing x unless x would in some circumstances suffer the change c. The principle cannot reasonably be applied to any case in which the 'impossibility' is a matter of the agent's motivation. The example of the 'physical impossibility' of jumping

[1] For another, cf. R. Taylor, op. cit.

thirty feet may seem to count against me, since this impossibility derives from the nature of the agent and a jump is not, like the change from lead to gold, an event 'brought about' indirectly. But this example seems only to be an instance of an argument from a natural impossibility to an impossibility for choice because the claim that it is impossible that I should jump thirty feet would normally be supported – and was, in the example, assumed to be supported – by reference to the inadequacies of my physique, fitness, training, etc., rather than to my motivation. Appeal would be made to my lack of capacity, rather than to my lack of will. People like me have tried and failed to jump very far, and their failure may indeed be explicable by the laws of mechanics. But a claim that 'it is impossible that Smith should jump twenty feet' *might* be supported, even if Smith is physically capable of jumping twenty feet, not by reference to his physique but by the argument that it would be out of character for him to exert himself, or that he regards athletics with contempt, or that it is against his religion to allow both feet to leave the ground at once. Now the determinist simply denies that there is a significant difference between the two cases. But there is a difference, and its significance should by now be evident. For in the one case the ultimate appeal is to trials and failures, and in the other case it is not, unless it is to trials and failures on our part to get Smith to put his ability to the test.

The view that there is no difference gets much of its popularity from two confusions. The first is a common misinterpretation of the difference between the evidence of physique on the one hand and the evidence of character and motivation on the other, as if it were merely the difference between physical aspects and mental aspects of the agent; as if anyone who insists on a difference is arbitrarily restricting the notion of an incapacity or inability to physical impossibilities, and is refusing to count psychological incapacities as real incapacities. Now of course it is true that mental abilities are important. It would be absurd to say of someone that he is capable of answering a complicated question in mathematics merely on the ground that he is physically capable of writing down the set of symbols that express the right answer. His ability will be a function of his skill at mathematics, he must not be suffering from a mental blackout and so on. But his ability to answer the question put to him does not depend on its being 'psychologically possible' that he should answer it, if this is supposed to mean that he must be an obedient pupil willing to answer, or the like. It is a gross misunderstanding of the relationship between capacity and will to equate it with the distinction between physical and mental capacities.

Secondly, it might be thought that physiology could show that our distinction between the case of Smith, who does not jump twenty feet because he cannot and that of Brown, who does not jump twenty feet because of his peculiar moral convictions, is without foundation. For it is likely that Brown's non-performance is explicable in physical terms, just as much as Smith's. Brown's moral convictions, we are assured, correspond to his brain state or the condition of his glands. It is surely arbitrary, the determinist will protest, to distinguish between the evidence of Smith's muscle-state that he cannot jump twenty feet, and the evidence of Brown's brain-state that he cannot jump twenty feet. But this protest, and the bogy of materialism, stems from the familiar misunderstanding of possibility for choice. The condition of Smith's muscles is seen to be relevant to what he can do because there is a significant correlation, not simply between muscle-states and performance or non-performance, but between muscle-states and success or failure. If nobody had ever tried to jump as far as he could, there would no doubt be an exceptionless correlation between every kind of muscular condition and the non-performance of the act of jumping twenty feet. Men would then presumably be ignorant of their jumping abilities, but this would not mean that they lacked them. However many observations, over however wide a variety of cases, a psychologist might make of men in a particular physiological state who refuse, for example, to eat meat on account of their moral convictions, the hypothesis that such men *cannot* eat meat, while it may be plausible, remains untested until the psychologist finds a suitable subject who is prepared to put it to the test. This is not to say that the state of a man's brain may not be extremely important in determining his capacities. For, of course, trials might show that a certain brain condition really does prevent a man from jumping twenty feet, or from standing up for long periods, or from being good at mathematics. But without actual trials by people in that state there can be no direct reason for associating a brain-state, or any physical condition, with an incapacity.

The introduction of the notion of 'necessary conditions' into the determinist's argument, while making it more complex and, perhaps, formidable, adds nothing to its real cogency; although it demonstrates that one strength of determinism is the number of guises in which it can appear. As there are different kinds of possibility, so there are different kinds of 'necessary condition'. The proposition that A is a necessary condition for *doing B*, is a proposition that is tested by trying to do B without A, and can be supported by reference to failures to do B without A. It is a mistake to think that my deciding to do an action, or my having a reason or motive for doing it, could be necessary conditions of this kind for my doing it. On the other hand, there is a sense in which decisions, wishes, motives and reasons can be regarded as 'necessary conditions' for events: for example, it may be a necessary condition for peace in Vietnam that President Ho Chi Minh should have a reason for wanting peace. But the absence of this condition, while it might present an obstacle to President Johnson in obtaining peace, would hardly do the same to Ho Chi Minh. That would be like calling a club exclusive on the ground that a necessary condition for joining is wanting to join.

If all that is necessary for water to boil is present in nature, then the water will boil. But although all that is necessary for me to boil water is present in my kitchen, I need not boil water. This illustration of freewill is a demonstration, not of indeterminism in my kitchen, but of two kinds of 'necessary condition'.

3. ON NOT BEING ABLE TO HELP IT: A DISCUSSION OF THE RELATIONSHIP BETWEEN POWER AND RESPONSIBILITY

I shall now consider some apparent counter-examples to my thesis. I have argued that the ultimate verification of attributions of personal power, and of any proposition that some state of the agent or some set of circumstances in which he is placed is a factor determining his ability to do an action, is by reference to trials, that is, successes and failures; that this verification cannot be explained on the model of stimulus and response, or antecedent and consequent conditions; and that the difference between power and act corresponds to the difference between 'Can I?', and 'Shall I?' The determinist may object that we know of a man who is sound asleep that he cannot run a mile or give a lecture, although a man in that state never tries to run a mile or give a lecture. We know that he cannot do so, it may be said, not because there is no point in his deliberating what to do, but because he *cannot* deliberate on what to do; not because any trial will be a failure, but because he cannot try. And there are other cases in which a lack of the ability to do something may seem to consist in a lack of the ability even to consider doing it. The same kind of case, of course, also supplies standard objections to the theory, different from our own, that 'he could' means 'he would, if he tried'.

A man who is a little drunk may say things that he regrets later, and that he would not have said if he had 'been himself'. He is physically capable of saying anything – even 'Red lorry, yellow lorry' – or nothing. He has not become stupid – perhaps his remarks are wittier than usual. He would have been able to restrain himself, if he had tried to, but he just felt like telling some home truths. Yet can he not plead that he was *not* really in control of his tongue, that he 'could not help it'? Or suppose that he is provoked, his nationality is insulted, he gets angry and he throws a bottle. This man, it may be argued, is surely not responsible for his actions. It seems little good pointing out that others have refrained in similar circumstances – perhaps they were not so patriotic, or hot-tempered, or affected by drink. It seems no good pointing out that if he had tried not to throw the bottle, he would have succeeded. The whole trouble was that what he tried to do, and succeeded in doing, was to throw the bottle. In this case, the argument may continue, 'He could have refrained, if he had tried' would be a genuine conditional; although not, it should be noticed, on the grounds that the trying would have bestowed the ability, but on the ground that a situation in which the man would have tried to refrain, would also have been a situation in which he would have been able to refrain. The implication will be, that if the ability to do something waits upon character, mood, will and the rest here, why should we not come to the conclusion, on reflection, that it always does. If a nationalistic upbringing and strong drink can *prevent* a man from taking an insult lying down, why should not a pacifistic, internationalist and teetotal upbringing *prevent* another man from hitting those who insult his nationality? It is arbitrary (we may be told) to distinguish between the one man's lack of control of his actions, and the other's 'self-control'. Is not our chief reason for doing so perhaps merely that we disapprove of hitting people? Or the accident that one man, in a different condition, comes to regret his action?

Another favourite example in discussion is that of so-called brain-washing. The prisoner is captured in a state of patriotic determination to do nothing to harm his country, if he can avoid it. After 'brain-washing', he is released to spy against his country, not because he is being made to do so, but because he now wants to do so. To give way to brain-washing is to allow one's motivation to be changed, not to do something in spite of one's motivation. Yet the victim can hardly be held fully responsible for his actions or his views, and does not deserve the honorific title of 'free agent'. He 'could not help' being converted and he 'cannot help' thinking the way he does. But, the determinist will add, is he so different from the rest of us? Is not everyone influenced by background, education and the subtle, or not so subtle, pressures of their society? Few in Russia are pro-capitalist, few in America are pro-communist. But in any case, the bare possibility of brain-washing, post-hypnotic suggestion, and subliminal advertising, not to speak of paranoia and madness in which the will is affected, seems to create difficulties for our account of the relation between capacity and will.

We cannot here discuss in detail all the issues raised by these cases and the wide range which they represent and on which the determinist can draw. We shall mention a few, but two things need to be said first. One is that 'I could not help it' and 'He could not do otherwise' are used very loosely as what we might call 'excusing expressions', even when the excuse offered is not really that the agent was literally incapable of doing anything else. We have already discussed the case of a man acting under a threat, of whom we might say that he 'can only do one thing', simply because it would be unreasonable to choose the alternative possibility. 'Ordinary language' is a poor guide.

The second point is a corollary of the first: there really are other reasons for excusing an action than that the agent could not have done anything else, and there are other grounds for talking of diminished responsibility, or lack of 'freedom', than the absence of possibilities for choice. It is chiefly a failure to appreciate these two points that makes the kinds of cases I have mentioned plausible counter arguments to my thesis.

Austin, in his paper 'A Plea for Excuses', suggests the distinction between justifying an action and otherwise excusing it as the first great division among excuses or kinds of extenuation: 'In one defense, briefly, we accept responsibility but deny that [the action] was bad: in the other, we admit that it was bad, but don't accept full, or any responsibility.' This dichotomy may seem very obvious, but it is overlooked in the deterministic interpretation that we imagined being given of our case of the man who threw the bottle. Certainly we might tend to find excuses for such a man, but one of them at least would very likely be that his reaction to provocation, if a little excessive, was not entirely unjustified or improper, or at least that the opinion that it was a proper reaction is not entirely unreasonable. The plea of provocation also implies that the victim must share the blame or responsibility for what occurred. Cases of shared responsibility suggest that Austin is not quite right in linking justification so rigidly with acceptance of responsibility: to justify an action is certainly not to disclaim it, but justification may involve disclaiming some responsibility for what occurred. One kind of case is when bad advice is given and taken. Indeed, sometimes the adviser must take all the blame. If my doctor advises walking when he should advise rest, he must bear the responsibility for the walks I take. My defence is a justification, and it would be absurd to say that my doctor really took the walks, or that I did not really take them: I should disclaim responsibility, but not the act itself. None of this implies that the agent who is excused, literally could not have done otherwise. Moreover, to return to the bottle-thrower, we would not accept the taunts as an excuse because, or simply because, they happened to *cause* the man's reaction, but because they were provoking.

Admittedly – and this is why this particular case is an awkward one – there are likely to be other excuses for the bottle-thrower. The simple fact of anger can seem a mitigation. It is sometimes said that it is inexcusable to hit a child in anger, but it is also said that what is inexcusable is to hit a child not in anger. But once again, to offer this excuse in such a case does not imply a real inability to do anything else. Moreover, while anger may prevent us from doing some things, it is not the kind of thing that could ever literally prevent us from trying to act in a particular way. Angry men do still think, and while it may not be absurd for an angry man to decide to avoid his colleagues, on the ground that he could not hide his anger from them, it would be absurd for him to argue that, since in his state he cannot try to hide his anger, he will not try. Moods, too, do not compel us to make particular decisions, but, on the contrary, can be taken into account in deliberation: we can recognise that a fit of depression is not the best time to write home, although, if we had written, our mood would have served as some excuse for a gloomy tone.

In an emotional state we tend to act thoughtlessly, impulsively, without deliberation, but it does not follow that we are incapable of deliberation. For what would then be the point of the commonplace injunction to stop and think, to count twenty and so on, in such situations, and how could it ever be effective, as it sometimes is? Emotion may excuse, but for more subtle reasons than that a man in an emotional state 'cannot act otherwise'. A man has just heard of the death of his friend – he may be excused for a harsh rejoinder to an inept criticism of the friend's work. A man has just come from the glories of the Doge's Palace – he may be excused for thinking it superior to the Parthenon. 'Excusable' does not mean the same as 'unavoidable', here or anywhere else.[1] But as we make our excuses, we are understandably inclined to present our rage, grief, elevation or desire metaphorically as forces which, so to speak, did our action for us. The determinist, with his false metaphysical preconceptions, exhorts us to take this fainthearted metaphor too seriously.

Perhaps the biggest cliché of popular determinism is the doctrine that we are all creatures of heredity, upbringing and environment, and of the character that these have bestowed on us. It is, as I have said, absurd to present a man's character as proof that he could not do otherwise, but it is not absurd to mention his background as an excuse of some kind for both his character and his actions. But once more, it is not an excuse of the form, 'It is not in his power to be, or to do, any-

---

[1] It may prevent a misunderstanding if it is made plain that these cases are not cases of something excusable 'by definition', or in virtue of 'ordinary usage', but are examples of how something can be said to be excusable, without the implication that it is unavoidable.

thing else.' People can and do escape from the ways of thought and behaviour of their youth, reflect on the real extent of the beloved father's virtue, recognise for themselves in the once-admired teacher a man of small prejudices, and diagnose and control in themselves tendencies they despise in their grandfathers. Of course, heredity and upbringing often do cause genuine incapacities, and a social situation can literally restrict opportunities. When we fail to understand physicists, we mutter apologetic things about a classical education. But this obvious point is hardly at issue.

It is a crude misinterpretation even of the Freudian unconscious, and the dark forces therein, as something that compels us to do things, making alternatives impossible. There may be hysterical incapacities, but these do not represent the only kind of influence the unconscious can have. If it is not implausibly said that wars have a source in the death-wish and that the patriot's war-fever is a perversion of sexual desire, then war is presented as an understandable phenomenon but not as an inevitable one. On the contrary, seeing martial ardour in this light may help us to see it as something to be rejected.

There is a significant distinction between excuses that can be offered when the action is just about to be performed, and those that only become available after it has been performed. The plea that nothing else is possible, like justification, falls clearly into the first class. But the appeal to background and upbringing falls as clearly into the second; except when it is brought in to excuse a genuine incapacity, like the inability to drive, or when it is really an appeal to past experience or past advice in justification of an attitude, like a suspicion of pawnbrokers or a belief that honesty does not pay.

Pleas of ignorance, which are not unconnected with the appeal to 'background', raise complicated issues. Not knowing how to do something is also, roughly speaking, not being able to do it.[1] But there are other kinds of ignorance or lack of awareness. 'I did not know that there was a fire extinguisher', 'It did not occur to me that there would be a fire extinguisher', 'It did not occur to me to look for a fire

---

[1] Not always: 'I did not know how to work the extinguisher' can be met with 'Could you not read the instructions?' or 'Did it not occur to you to press the button?' Both questions imply 'You could have worked it', but hardly 'You knew how to.'

extinguisher' are all different excuses for not using the fire extinguisher, but none of them imply inability to use it. This may be seen from the possible excuse, 'It did not occur to me until later that I could have used it.' It is also, obviously, possible to inform someone of what he is already capable of doing. And to suggest courses of action to someone is not to make them possible for him. Unless they are possible, it is pointless to suggest them. Nevertheless, 'It did not occur to me' can often be some kind of excuse, largely depending on the probabilities, even if it is as often sadly inadequate.

The first would-be counter-example that we considered, of a man sound asleep, is an interesting one. There is in fact something very odd about saying of a sleeping man that he cannot walk, on the ground that he is asleep and so cannot try to walk: as odd as it would be to regard sleepwalking as the exercise of a capacity or skill. It seems that it is wrong to assert *or* deny that an unconscious man has the power to do something, except in the straightforward sense in which we can see whether he has it when he wakes up. In this respect, except that he is not past waking, a sleeping man is not too different from a dead one. Our thesis that it is ultimately only by trials that we know what is within our power is hardly refuted by the argument that we know that a dead man, or, for that matter, a pillar-box, cannot walk, although neither has ever tried to walk. The philosophical explanation of the distinction between what does and what does not act intentionally may be a large question, but it is pretty clear on which side of the line corpses and pillar-boxes lie. It is absurd to propose either as things that cannot walk because they cannot try to walk; that is, cannot see whether they can walk. Perhaps some extreme cases of madness are to be approached in the same way. On the other hand, many of the insane, like the kleptomaniac who haunts department stores and books on freewill, may have more possibilities open to them than is popularly supposed.

Not surprisingly, since the interpretation of borderline cases keeps the pot boiling in metaphysics, the kinds of examples I have discussed may raise problems outside our sort of academic inquiry. Where the boundaries of legal responsibility should lie, the extent to which criminals are psychopaths, how much allowance should be made for 'background' or for stupidity, what attitude to take towards the victims of brain-washing, are all real questions, worthy of serious consideration. One of the most important things we can ask about ourselves and others, is how far we have accepted, without serious reflection, inadequate goals presented to us since our early life, and how far we have accepted as unavoidable what is not. The pretensions of the determinist to settle these questions for us with a single, sweeping conclusion are not tolerable: it is as grotesque for a law reformer to attempt a definition of legal responsibility, or to advocate doing away with the concept altogether, armed with the arguments of metaphysical determinism, as it would be for the designer of a rocket to pay attention to Zeno's arguments for the impossibility of motion. It may seem to be an important difference that we cannot seriously act as if motion is impossible, whereas we can act as if no man could ever have acted differently; for example, by adjusting our treatment of criminals accordingly. The difference is illusory. No one could consistently believe that, or act as if, there is never more than one course of action open to him. We can refrain from blaming, perhaps, but not from deciding. Yet this analogy provides no reason at all for treating determinism as a contemptible metaphysical theory. We need to be sure that we can supply not only a convincing refutation but also a full explanation of his argument, before we can afford to be condescending even to Zeno.

4. ON THE MEANING OF WORDS LIKE 'CAN'

Metaphysical determinism characteristically arises out of the general conflation of the possible with the actual that I have called 'actualism'. Some philosophers who aim to expose the dilemma between metaphysical determinism and indeterminism as an unreal one, see in actualism the one major misconception. Consequently they assume that no more is required in order to refute determinism than a general understanding of the distinction between potentiality and actualisation, which they imagine can be achieved by a general explanation of powers as 'dispositional' properties, and of unrealised potentialities by unfulfilled conditionals. Nowell-Smith and Stevenson,[1] for example, treat the determinist as, primarily, a sceptic about unexercised dispositions and counterfactual conditionals.

[1] v. Nowell-Smith, op. cit., pp. 276-7; Stevenson, op. cit., pp. 299-300.

We have seen that scepticism can be a source of actualism, and so of metaphysical determinism. But we have also discovered that the power of choice cannot be treated as a dispositional property or natural power, and consequently that no general all-embracing explanation of the potentiality/actuality distinction is possible. This difference in kind may be either obscured or exploited, or both obscured and exploited, in an argument for determinism. It is, of course, ignored in any version of the 'Basic Argument', which passes directly from an argument about natural possibility and power to a conclusion about personal power. This is a flaw in that argument. On the other hand, the difference is often exploited in response to any attempt to refute such an argument by means of an explanation of the powers of people as analogous to the powers of things. For, as I have stressed, the peculiar character of possibility for choice, when it is not understood, can generate a special and an especially plausible form of actualism. Consequently it is wrong to see the source of metaphysical determinism in a single, sweeping mistake. There are separable, if not always separate strands in the dialectic of determinism.

Moore picks up one thread in the tangle with his claim that 'could' is ambiguous, although people have failed to realise it. This is the suggestion that I shall now consider, although I shall be concerned with the nature of the differences between kinds of possibility in general, rather than with Moore's particular thought that there is one sense in which it may be true that nothing ever could have been other than it is, and another sense in which it is certainly false. At any rate, Moore's approach seems to rest on the possibility that words like 'can', 'possible', 'power', 'necessary', are actually ambiguous, and that the determinist has failed to recognise this 'simply because it does not occur to people that words often are ambiguous' (op. cit., p. 130). The suggestion is that the determinist is guilty of the fallacy of equivocation.

My argument that the determinist characteristically confuses possibility for choice with other kinds of possibility might seem to commit me to an acceptance of this suggestion, but considerations quite consistent with what I have said so far can in fact be brought against it. It must be conceded that determinists *may* exploit, or overlook, what is certainly an ambiguity. It is fairly common for a determinist to use a sentence that is capable of expressing either of two kinds of possibility-statement, as if it can express only one. For example, Hume argues that 'when we see a person free from strong motives, we suppose a possibility of his acting or forbearing'. The main clause of this sentence is certainly ambiguous, since it may mean either that we suppose that the man could act or forbear, or that we suppose it uncertain whether he will act or forbear. Hume wants to identify these two different things, and an ambiguous expression helps his argument. It is also probable that he was himself misled by such ambiguities. It hardly needs saying that examples of this kind of equivocation commonly occur in the freewill controversy.

Moore's suggestion, however, is not that the determinist is sometimes misled by ambiguous sentences or remarks, but that he is always misled by ambiguous words, namely 'could' and, presumably, cognate words. It is not so easy to say whether Moore is right. For if it is sometimes unclear whether a sentence is ambiguous, it is often still less clear how the senses of a word like 'can' should be counted. The question arises whether 'can' is ambiguous at all. It is often assumed that the sense of words can be treated as a simple function of the sense of sentences: for example, that it is at least a sufficient condition for the ambiguity of a word if, on some occasions of its use, it is synonymous with a word or expression with which it is not synonymous on other occasions of its use; 'synonymy' being the relation between words, expressions and sentences that are interchangeable without alteration of the sense of what is said, i.e., in the case of individual words, without alteration of the sense of the sentence in which they occur on some particular occasion of its use. Thus, on some occasions of its use, 'if' may be replaced, without changing the sense of the sentence, by 'provided that', and at other times, by 'even if'. Accordingly it would be taken to have at least two senses. By a similar argument 'possible' would also be ambiguous, because it is sometimes interchangeable with 'logically possible' and sometimes not; or because it can sometimes be replaced by 'not necessary ... not', but at other times must be replaced by 'not certain ... not' if the sense of the utterance is to be retained.

Quite apart from this possibility of replacement by a variety of words and expressions, it may seem plausible that 'can' and cognate words must be supposed to have a variety of senses corresponding to the very different kinds of statement they can be used in making: 'Can my mother knit?', 'Can my mother be alive?',[1] 'You can run now (I give permission)', 'You can run now (the muscle is healed)', 'I cannot buy it now (the shops are shut)', 'I cannot buy it now (I have better things to do)', 'It cannot rain tonight (that would be too disappointing)', 'It cannot rain unless there are clouds', 'We cannot fly to the moon', 'We cannot square the circle.' The tendency to multiply senses may be increased by the philosophical explanation of meaning as 'use', as well as by the standard association of meaning with 'the method of verification'. It is an attractive characterisation of the variety of our list that its members exemplify different *uses* of 'can'.

These arguments are not, however, conclusive. For example, our inclination to agree that 'possible' sometimes means 'logically possible' and sometimes 'empirically possible' need not be taken as an indication that 'possible' is ambiguous, but simply that we often speak elliptically or – and this is the better way of putting it, since there are reasons for not representing the adverb as 'already there' or 'understood' in the original sentence – that the meaning of utterances containing 'possible' without either adverb can be made clearer by the addition of an appropriate adverb. If the ambiguity of the sentence 'It is possible to turn lead into gold' is due simply to this sort of inexplicitness, there is no need to blame it on a presumed ambiguity of 'possible'. That is to say, we can question the prevalent but really rather curious notion, that when a sentence is elliptical a particular word or expression in it somehow carries within its meaning what has been left out. Dictionaries actually list 'elliptical senses'. The *O.E.D.* lists such a 'sense' of *can*, in which it is said to be short for *can do*, e.g. 'I will do all I can' and 'He could no more.' But the separate treatment of these examples in the dictionary is surely no more than a device for setting out an idiom, and thereby performing one of the functions of a dictionary: it is idiomatic, in certain circumstances, to leave out infinitives after 'can', as after auxiliaries. This idiom cannot seriously be supposed to generate a separate sense of 'can', in which it means 'can do' (not to speak of senses for 'can walk', 'can talk', *ad infinitum*), any more than the same idiom generates separate senses of 'would', 'will', 'shall' and so on. 'Elliptical senses' are not really senses. Moore's own argument shows that this is a

---

[1] Example from *O.E.D.*, 'expressing contingency'.

point sometimes worth making in a philosophical context. For he suggests that, since we often mean by 'I could' no more than 'I could, if I wished', then 'could' is ambiguous, although it does not normally occur to us that it is. Moore's argument is in any case fundamentally mistaken at a philosophical level, since it presupposes that 'I could, if I wished' is conditional; but even if it were not, his point must be that we often use 'could' in elliptical sentences, although we do not realise that they are elliptical. He does not put it like this, presumably because, when the meaning of the sentence uttered on a particular occasion, 'I could do it', is further explained by the sentence 'I could do it, if I wished', he very oddly takes the explanation as the replacement of the word 'could' by the expression 'could, if I wished', rather than, simply, as an expansion of the original sentence, leaving 'could' just as it was.

It may, of course, be that the replacement of one word in a sentence, without alteration of the meaning of the sentence on some occasion of its use, is a genuine replacement and cannot be treated simply as an addition to, or expansion of the original sentence. The replacement of 'if' by 'even if' is a bogus replacement, and it provides no proof of a separate meaning of 'if'; any more than the ambiguity of the sentence 'On the supposition that he walks home, he will be hungry', which may or may not be used to mean '*Even* on the supposition . . .', provides proof of the ambiguity of 'on', or of 'supposition', or of 'on the supposition that'. The replacement of 'if' by 'provided that' is a real replacement. Nevertheless we cannot take it that the possibility of such genuine replacement on some occasions of its use, but not on others, proves that 'if' is ambiguous.

If we concentrate on certain kinds of example, the 'replacement rules' for ambiguity and synonymy may seem absolute. The word 'brush' may sometimes be replaced by the expression 'bushy tail', and sometimes not. The expression 'cousin of X' is sometimes replaceable by the expression 'child of a brother or sister of X's father or mother' and sometimes not. 'Brush' and 'Cousin', it seems, are thereby ambiguous. Nevertheless, other examples, with different kinds of words, show at least that this principle cannot be applied indiscriminately. 'He is no more' would normally mean the same as 'He is no longer *living*', and 'The house is no more', as 'The house is no longer *standing*', but the expression 'is no more' has the same meaning in both sentences: the 'is' of existence is not indefinitely ambiguous. Now just as 'is' or 'exists' performs the same general function, in whatever existence may consist for the particular kind of thing in question, so 'if' seems to perform the general function of introducing a 'condition or supposition' (*O.E.D.*), the protasis of a conditional, whether or not the conditional is of such a kind that the 'if' might have been replaced by the more explicit 'provided that', or by 'even if', or by 'although'.[1]

It follows from this explanation that the relation between 'if' and 'provided that' is not, after all, so much like that between 'brush' and 'bushy tail', the latter giving one of the senses of the former, as it is like the relation between 'tail' and 'brush' or 'bushy tail', the latter being more specific than the former. There is a difference, however. For if someone says of an animal 'It has a tail', no context, short of a prearranged code, could lead us to suppose that his utterance *means* 'It has a bushy tail': 'It has a tail' never means the same as 'It has a bushy tail.' But if someone says 'If you come late, you will get a seat', the context, or his tone of voice, may very well make it clear that what is meant is '*Even if* you come late . . .', or else '*Provided that* you come late . . .' It is this that can lead us to think that the first 'if' is ambiguous, whereas it is just not very explicit. 'Provided that' happens to be more explicit.

Another way of putting the difference is this. If someone uses the inexplicit sentence 'If you arrive late, you will get a seat' and we are not clear about his meaning, it is natural to get him to make clear whether he means that arriving late is a sufficient, or a necessary and sufficient condition for getting a seat, or that arriving late is not related to getting a seat at all. He must have meant one of these things – he cannot simply have meant something conditional but inexplicit. But it would be absurd to ask someone who says 'The lemur has a tail', whether he means by this that it has a bushy tail, or that it has a non-bushy tail. If 'It has a tail' is inexplicit, the speaker can mean something inexplicit, and has a perfect right to leave it inexplicit. Neverthe-

---

[1] 'Conditional' here must include conditional questions, commands, etc. 'Pseudo-conditionals' (*v.* above, e.g., pp. 119–124) will also need special discussion; even so, it is doubtful whether they need generate a special sense of 'if'. (Cf. Austin: *Philosophical Papers*, pp. 158–61.)

less this difference does not seem a good reason for convicting 'if' of ambiguity, or for denying that the possibility of replacing 'if' by 'provided that' on some occasions but not on others stems rather from the generality of its function, than from ambiguity.

Now if we here see the meaning of 'if' as lying in its general function of introducing a condition or supposition, we also have a powerful weapon against the argument that categorical differences between conditional statements must involve different senses of 'if'. 'If x is a raven, x is black' is ambiguous, because it might express either an *a priori* or an empirical proposition. A man could disagree with the former while assenting to the latter. It is tempting to think that if the sentence is ambiguous, then at least one word in it must be ambiguous, and 'if', or 'if ... then ...', may seem the best candidate. But the ambiguity of the sentence derives from its inexplicitness, not from the ambiguity of a particular word. Whichever meaning the sentence has, 'if' is performing its standard function. A sentence can be ambiguous although no word in it is ambiguous. We can prove this simply by replacing 'if' with 'on the supposition that'. The sentence is still ambiguous, but surely not because of an ambiguity of this expression.[1]

The view that 'if' is ambiguous may sometimes rest on the fact that the expression '$p \supset q$' can be read as 'q, if p'. The meaning of the symbol '$\supset$', it is said, is given in the appropriate truth-table; therefore at least one meaning of 'if' can be given in a truth-table. The question whether 'if' is ambiguous, it then seems, devolves on whether, fundamentally, this is *always* the meaning of 'if', and whether apparent divergences of conditional statements from a truth-functional structure can all be explained away. But against this argument, we can question whether the meaning of 'if', even when it does replace '$\supset$', is ever given in a truth-table. The relation of 'if' to '$\supset$' seems much the same as its relation to 'provided that'. It is simply less explicit or specific: in this case because '$\supset$' is a technical symbol generally and, perhaps, properly limited to a context which ensures a truth-functional interpretation of the whole expression. Truth and falsity may come into the question of the meaning of 'if', to the extent that conditional

---

[1] Cf. G. E. L. Owen: 'Aristotle on the Snares of Ontology' in *New Essays on Plato and Aristotle*, ed. Bambrough, pp. 74–5. Unfortunately Owen's examples are not entirely happy.

statements have at least one thing in common: *p and ~q* entails *~(if p, then q*). That may be why it is natural and proper to read both '$p \to q$' and '$p \supset q$' as '*If p, then q*', in spite of the difference, which it is pointless to deny, between material implication and strict implication, and between both kinds of statement and the kind of thing that would normally be meant by 'If the bough breaks, the cradle will fall.' That 'if' can be used in expressing them all may tell us something about its meaning, but not necessarily that it has many meanings.

The same kind of account can be given of 'can', 'possible' and so on. It is as difficult to state the function of 'can' as that of 'if', but it might be described figuratively as an 'allowing' function. 'Cannot', 'impossible' rule out, and it may be argued that this *same* 'ruling out' function is fulfilled whether we are ruling out propositions, events, things, kinds of performance or particular proposed actions or whatever, and whether an appropriate ground for the specific type of 'ruling out' is logical absurdity, past observation, past failure or practical reasoning. That 'It is possible that . . .' is replaceable only sometimes by 'It is not a law that . . . not . . .', only sometimes by 'It is not certain that . . . not . . .', only sometimes by 'It is not logically necessary that . . . not . . .' and only sometimes by 'It is practicable that . . .' may simply show that it functions in a wider, but no less unified field than any of these other expressions. Certainly, in every case we can apply such platitudinous principles as '*p* entails that *p* is possible' or ' "*p* is possible" does not entail *p*'.

The concept of possibility has, in all its applications, the same place in a simple network of concepts, the parts of which are related as contradictories, contraries and subcontraries. This is ensured by the difference between 'It is not possible that *p*' and 'It is possible that *p* is false.' Such a place is filled even by the permissive 'can', which is likely to be dubbed a special 'sense' just because it is not used in the expression of a proposition. 'You can go', meaning 'Go, if you wish', is the subcontrary of 'You need not go' or 'Do not go, if you do not want to go.' Their respective contradictories are 'Do not go' and 'Go' or 'You must go'. These inter-relationships cannot, of course, be supposed to tell us very much about the meaning of 'can', since modality is not essential to a difference between contradictories and contraries, or to the logical relationships of the 'Square of Opposition'. So much can be demonstrated by examples less controversial than the distinction between modality and mere totality, or universals of law and universals of fact. For 'x is completely red' and 'x is completely blue', as well as 'x is necessary' and 'x is impossible', are contraries rather than contradictories; while their respective contradictories, 'x is not completely red' and 'x is not completely blue' are related as subcontraries. Nevertheless, the Square of Opposition may remind us of a unity underlying the usage of 'can'.

It may seem that a dictionary is the highest authority on meanings, and dictionaries tend to suggest that most words have plenty of them. The *Oxford English Dictionary* certainly gives the impression that words acquire (and, less often, lose) senses as ships acquire barnacles, and that 'can' is no exception. As we have seen in the case of elliptical 'senses', the *O.E.D.* has an idiosyncratic notion of what constitutes a sense, a notion that may suit its particular purposes very well. There is no need to regard the variety that the dictionary displays as a variety of different senses, or the historical change that it unfolds as an accretion of new meanings. The list of 'senses' of 'can' may illustrate rather something of the process of the widening of an earlier meaning in a particular and intelligible direction. It is too complicated a matter to enter into here, but such an approach might help to deal with the interesting difficulties that beset the attempt made in the *O.E.D.* to count the senses of 'can' in a precise way.[1] This certainly seems the most sensible way to take the history of 'and', which comes from a word meaning, roughly, *with* or *beside*. The stratification of senses and examples in the *O.E.D.* reasonably suggests that it might once have been more natural to use 'and' to conjoin substantives than to connect adjectives or sentences: 'Men *and* women filled the room' might once have seemed more natural than 'Men filled one room *and* women filled the other.' Yet 'and' is now an absolutely general conjunction, and there seems no point in attributing different senses to it in each of these sentences.

If we talk of each dictionary item or each valid philosophical distinction as marking off a 'use' of a word like 'can', 'if', 'possible',

---

[1] E.g. the distinction between sense 4 and sense 6 of 'can' will not survive much reflection. This is not because these 'senses' merge into each other in borderline cases. Even the reasons for regarding them as different points on a continuum are suspect.

'probable', we should recognise that these 'uses' may be related rather as the use of a spade to dig swedes is related to its use in digging potatoes. Perhaps our chief complaint against the multiplication of senses is that it draws again, and may pretend to explain, distinctions that are better drawn in other ways; taking from us a valuable tool, perhaps the best and most natural tool for expressing the unity behind the variety that appears at the propositional level. We need to be able to state that our interest in possibility is an interest in one thing, as well as in many things, and to explain why our concern for 'can' does not extend to cans of beans.

The suggestion that we should see in a generic use of 'can' the unity lying behind what may, from various points of view, seem distinct specific uses, offers one way of doing without an unhelpful and messy proliferation of meanings. But uses of 'can' may be associated in other ways than by a general similarity. 'I can roll this' is readily made passive without change in meaning: 'This can be rolled by me.' There is not much difference between the passive 'This can be rolled' and 'This can be made to roll', or the intransitive, 'This can roll.'[1] We have moved from talking of personal power to talking of natural power, but surely by a route sufficiently painless for us to doubt whether the grammatical transformation involved cannot now be performed without alteration in the sense of 'can'; even if the temptation which existed to allow such a transformation may help to explain how 'can' lost its original, narrow sense of 'know' or 'know how'.

We cannot rely on dictionary distinctions and etymology to tell us how to count meanings, but they are not therefore to be despised. 'Can' has come a long way since it was used almost exclusively to attribute knowledge skills to people, if it can now express logical possibility and contingency, what is practicable and what is tolerable. To recognise this progress is to be aware of differences, some of which have been of the greatest importance to us in our inquiry. It is true that etymology proves nothing in philosophy, but it may draw attention to what is significant.

---

[1] There is some difference, of course. But it is interesting that this is not nearly as striking as the difference between 'John can be rolled' and 'John can roll'. Cf. the Lockean suggestion that things have only 'passive powers', but people have 'active powers' as well.

If I am correct in my conclusion that 'could' is not ambiguous, it will follow that the determinist is not guilty of equivocation of the kind that Moore attributes to him. Yet this constitutes no defence of determinism, since none of my criticisms have required that 'could' should be ambiguous: nor, really, do Moore's suggestions require it. Determinism is wrong, even if the argument for it does not hinge on a verbal confusion of quite this kind. My method has been to investigate the different sorts of proposition that something is possible, and their interrelations. That the word 'possible' may not be ambiguous is irrelevant to my contentions.

This may seem a bathetic conclusion to a discussion of the meaning of 'can', for it would seem to make that discussion pointless and redundant. But it is generally a good thing to know what one is talking about. It may be a good thing to know that this inquiry into the diverse nature of possibility has not been an inquiry into different meanings of 'possible'.

Bibliography

BOOKS

Anson's Law of Contract, 20th ed., Oxford University Press, 1945.
Ayer, A. J., *Philosophical Essays*, Macmillan, 1959.
Bradley, F. H., *The Principles of Logic*, Oxford University Press, 1922.
Bradley, F. H., *Ethical Studies*, O.U.P., 1927.
Carroll, Lewis, *Sylvie and Bruno Concluded* in *Complete Works of Lewis Carroll*, Nonesuch, 1939.
Cranston, M., *Freedom: A New Analysis*, Longmans, 1954.
Geach, P., *Mental Acts*, Routledge and Kegan Paul, 1960.
Hampshire, S., *Thought and Action*, Chatto and Windus, 1959.
Hartmann, N., *Ethics* (trans. Coit), Allen and Unwin, 1926.
Hobbes, T., *Elements of Philosophy*, in Molesworth's edition of Hobbes, London, 1841.
Hobbes, T. and Bramhall, *Questions concerning Liberty, Necessity and Chance*, Molesworth's edition, London, 1841.
Hume, D., *A Treatise of Human Nature*, ed. Selby-Bigge, Oxford, 1888.
Hume, D., *An Enquiry concerning the Human Understanding*, ed. Selby-Bigge, Oxford, 1902.
Johnson, W. E., *Logic*, Cambridge University Press, 1921.
Keynes, J. M., *A Treatise on Probability*, Macmillan, 1921.
Kneale, W., *Probability and Induction*, O.U.P., 1949.
Locke, J., *An Essay concerning Human Understanding*, ed. Yolton, Dent, 1961 (Everyman Library).
Meldon, A. I., *Free Action*, Routledge and Kegan Paul, 1961.
Mill, J. S., *A System of Logic*, Longmans, 1959 imp.
Moore, G. E., *Ethics*, O.U.P., 1947 (Home University Library).
Nowell-Smith, P. H., *Ethics*, Penguin Books, 1965 imp.
Ryle, G., *The Concept of Mind*, Hutchinson, 1949.
Schlick, M., *Problems of Ethics* (trans. Rynin), Dover, 1962.
Stevenson, C. L., *Ethics and Language*, Yale, 1944.
Strawson, P. F., *Introduction to Logical Theory*, Methuen, 1952.

Taylor, C., *The Explanation of Behaviour*, Routledge and Kegan Paul, 1964.
Taylor, R., *Metaphysics*, Prentice-Hall, 1963.
Wittgenstein, L., *Tractatus Logico-Philosophicus* (trans. Ogden and Richards), Routledge and Kegan Paul, 1922.
Wittgenstein, L., *The Blue and Brown Books*, Blackwell, 1958.

ARTICLES

Austin, J. L., 'Ifs and Cans' in Austin, *Philosophical Papers*, Oxford University Press, 1961.
Austin, J. L., 'A Plea for Excuses' in Austin, *Philosophical Papers*, O.U.P., 1961.
Broad, C. D., 'Determinism, Indeterminism and Libertarianism' in Broad, *Ethics and the History of Philosophy*, Routledge and Kegan Paul, 1952.
Carnap, R., 'The Two Concepts of Probability' in Feigl and Sellars (eds.), *Readings in Philosophical Analysis*, Appleton-Century-Crofts, 1949.
Ebersole, F. B., 'Free Choice and the Demands of Morals', *Mind*, 1952.
Hampshire, S., 'Subjunctive Conditionals', *Analysis*, 1948.
Hart, H. L. A., 'The Ascription of Responsibility and Rights', *Proceedings of the Aristotelian Society*, 1948–9.
Mabbott, J. D., 'Freewill and Punishment' in Lewis (ed.), *Contemporary British Philosophy: 3rd Series*, Allen and Unwin, 1956.
Mackay, D. M., 'On the Logical Indeterminacy of Free Choice', *Mind*, 1960.
Owen, G. E. L., 'Aristotle on the Snares of Ontology' in Bambrough (ed.), *New Essays on Plato and Aristotle*, Routledge and Kegan Paul, 1965.
Popper, K. R., 'Indeterminism in Quantum Physics', *British Journal for Philosophy of Science*, vol. I, nos 2 & 3.
Stout, A. K., 'Freewill and Responsibility', *P.A.S.*, 1937.
Urmson, J. O., 'Two of the Senses of "probable"', *Analysis*, 1957.
Wiggins, D., 'Identity-Statements' in Butler (ed.), *Analytical Philosophy: 2nd Series*, Blackwell, 1965.

Index

Ability, 114; see also Possibility (1) and (2)
Actions,
  prediction of, see Prediction
  hierarchy of, 101
  habitual, 108–9
  and accomplishment, 111, 117–18
  and choosing, trying etc., Ch. 7, sects. 3 and 6 passim
  abortive, 144–5
  intentional, 117–18, 130, 133, 145–6, 168
Actualism, 6–7, 10, 15–17, 59, 62–3, 67–8, 77, 80, Ch. 5, sect. 4 passim, 102, 122, 125, 169–70
Advice, 141, 151, 153, 165–8
Agents,
  transcendent, 5
  inanimate, 89
  and patients, 96
  hierarchy of, 100
Ambiguity, 8–11, Ch. 3, sect. 3 passim, Ch. 8, sect. 4 passim; see also Senses, multiplication of
Analysis, 55, 69–70, 87–9, 144
Anger, 165–6
Anson's Law of Contract, 22
Austin, J. L., 119, 122–4, 137, 149, 165, 174
Available evidence, see Probability
Avoidability, 125–6, 133, 166
Ayer, A. J., 149

Basic Argument, 1–3, 5–10, 102, 170
Baker *v.* Hopkins, 22
Behaviourism, 131, 142

Borderline cases, 85, 100, 168, 177
Bradley, F. H., 70
Brain-washing, 164, 168
Bramhall, Bishop, 103
Broad, C. D., 4, 10, 121

'Can',
  tense of, 33–4
  etymology of, see Etymology
  alleged negativity of, 110–12, 135, 148–9
  permissive, 111, 172, 176
  mood of, 123–4
  in moral context, 135–6, 143
  meaning of, 127, 135, Ch. 8, sect. 4 passim
  see also Possibility
Capacities, general, Ch. 6 passim
Carnap, R., 42–5, 50–1
Carroll, Lewis, 122
Causal properties, 75, 83, 88–9, 107–8, 114–16, 127, 143; see also Dispositions
Causation,
  and freewill, 1–2, 27
  Hume on, 6, 56–9, 63–4
  Mill on, 78
  universal, 3–4, 94–5
Causes, efficient and underlying, 81–2
Certainty, see Possibility (3) and Uncertainty
Character, 4, 108, 126–7, 136–8, 153–8, 160, 163, 166–7
Choice,
  freedom of, 4, 120–1

Choice—*contd.*
  possibility for, *see* Possibility (1)
  'contra-causal', 4
  nature of, 135–7
  and analysis of possibility, Ch. 7, sects. 2–4 *passim*
  see also Decision *and* Deliberation
Circumstance, *see* Intrinsic and extrinsic properties
Common sense, 7–8, 78, 89
Compulsion, moral, 156–8
Conditional mood, *see* Subjunctive
Conditionals, *see* Hypotheticals
Constraint, absence of, 149; *see also* Prevention
Contradictories and contraries, 176–7

Death, 168
Decision,
  prediction of, *see* Prediction
  unavoidability of, 169
  see also Choice *and* Deliberation
Defeasibility, 148–9
Deliberation, 141, 143–4, 151–7, 163, 166; *see also* Decision
Descartes, 58, 86
Determinism, Ch. 1 *passim*, 14, 18, 26–32, 55, 67–8, 80, Ch. 5, sects. 4 and 5 *passim*, 102, 105–6, 120–2, 125–7, 147, 153, Ch. 8, sects. 2 and 3 *passim*, 169–71, 179
Dictionary, Oxford English, 9, 72, 172–3, 177–8
Difficulty, 147; *see also* Obstacles
Dispositionalism, 116–17, Ch. 6, sect. 3 *passim*, Ch. 7, sects. 4 and 5 *passim*
Dispositions,
  simple and complex, 110
  see also Causal properties, Dispositionalism *and* Character
Drunken man, 163–5

Effort, 129–30; *see also* Trying
Ellipsis, alleged,
  in probability statements, 19–26, 43–6
  in particular posssibility statements, 76, 93
  in ascriptions of power to people, 121
Elliptical senses, alleged, 172–3
Emotions, 166
Empirical possibility, *see* Possibility (2)
Empiricism, 56, 60, 68
Episodes, 107
Epistemology, 7, 37, Ch. 4 *passim*, 140, 148
Equivocation, fallacy of, 8–11, 170–171
Essence, 57, 82, 87; *see also* Nature (of a thing) *and* Intrinsic and extrinsic properties
Etymology, 54, 144, 177–8
Evidence,
  available, *see* Probability
  specificatory and statistical, 47
  directly and indirectly relevant, 73–4, 76–7
  see also Induction
Excuses, 136, 149, 155–6, Ch. 8, sect. 3 *passim*
Excusing expressions, 164
Exercise, *see* Possibility (1) *and* (2) *and* Actualism
Existence, 173–4
Experience, past, 37, 40–1, 59–60, 63–6, 69, 73–4; *see also* Induction
Experiment, *see* Tests *and* Trying
Explanation,
  and natural possibility, Ch. 4 *passim*
  of action, 2–5, 124, 140–1, 155–161, Ch. 8, sect. 3 *passim*
Extenuation, 165, *see also* Excuses
Extrinsic properties, *see* Intrinsic and extrinsic properties

Fact and law, 77–9, 177
Failure and success, 113, 117–18, 134, Ch. 7, sect. 6 *passim*, 160–3, 176; *see also* Trying
Falsifiability, 34, 63, 75, 134–5, 140, 147–9
Fatalism, 154
Fluke, 132–3
Fondness (fond of), 116–17, 135–6
Foreseeability, 22, 25
Freedom, 5, 103, 120, 126, 149, 164
Freewill, *see* Possibility (1) *and* Indeterminism
Frequency, relative, 42–3

Geach, P. T., 70
Genus, *see* Species

Habits, 108–10
Hampshire, S., 30, 70, 124
Hart, H. L. A., 149
Hartmann, N., 90
Heed, 109
Heredity, 166–7
Hobbes, 5, 8, 10, 96, 103, 105, 120
Hume, 6–7, 10, 15–18, 35–7, 39, 55–9, 62–70, 77, 120, 143, 149, 156
Hypotheticals,
    and possibility for choice, 10–11, Chs. 6 and 7 *passim*
    and natural possibility, Ch. 4, sects. 4 and 5 *passim*, Ch. 5 *passim*, 103–4, 110–12, 120–1, 124–5, 127–8, 139–40
    and dispositional properties, *see* Causal properties *and* Dispositions
    counterfactual, 70–5, 125–6, 135, 169
    subjunctive, 70–5, 124
    specific and unspecific, 75, 98, 107, 112, 128
    logical and grammatical, 136, 139, *see also* Pseudo-conditionals
    particular, 92
    open, 107
    eccentric, 134–5
    with impossible antecedent, 87–8
    consequential and inferential, 80–81, 98, 122

Identity, 53, 84
Ignorance, pleas of, 167–8
Indeterminism, Ch. 1 *passim*, 27, 94–5, 103, 105–6, 126, 151, 153, 162
Induction,
    and probability, 24, 43
    and natural possibility, Ch. 4 *passim*, 84, 140
    and possibility for choice, 37, 140, 146–50, 160–1
Inference-tickets, 140–1
Intelligence, 108–10, 126–7, 142
Intention,
    expressions of, 32–3, 49, 153
    and trying, 130–3, 145–6, 168
    and character, 155
Intentional action, *see* Actions
Intrinsic and extrinsic properties (or conditions), 52–3, 82–4, Ch. 5, sect. 3 *passim*, 90–3, 97, 99, 103–5, 115–16, 125, 142

Justification,
    of actions, 23, 30
    and extenuation, 165, 167

Keynes, J. M., 17–26, 46–7
Kleptomaniac, 168
Kneale, W., 19, 44

Language, appeal to, 8–9, 54, 94–6, 121–2, 155–6, 164, 166
Lawcourts, 22, 25, 143–4, 149
Laws of nature, 2, 12, Ch. 4, sect. 5 *passim*, 94, 160
Legislation, 143, 168–9
Liability (liable to), 112–14
Libertarianism, *see* Indeterminism
Liberty, hypothetical, 120, 122

Likely', 54
Luck, 118

Mabbott, J. D., 143, 149
MacKay, D. M., 30-2
Madness, 164, 168
Magic, 81, 99
Material implication, 134, 175-6
Materialism, 161
Meaning, 8-9, 23, 49, 59, 67, 81, 94-5, 98-9, 127, 135, 142-3, 148-9, Ch. 8, sect. 4 *passim*; see also Ambiguity *and* Senses, multiplication of
Means to ends, 126, 129-32, 142-3, 145, 152-3, 159-60
Mechanism, 3-5
Melden, A. I., 70, 131
Mill, J. S., 78, 93, 120-1
Mistakes, deliberate, 117
Mood, subjunctive, see Subjunctive
Moods (states of mind), 138, 166
Moore, G. E., 7-11, 14-15, 30, 36, 94-5, 121, 170-2, 179
Moral discourse, see 'Ought implies can'
Motives, 3-4, 116, 119, 125, 135, 148, 153-7, 160, 162, 164

Nature (of a thing), 52-3, 60, 69, 84-7, 90-1, 103-5; see also Intrinsic and extrinsic properties
Necessary conditions, 87, 89-91, 96-7, 99-100, 122, 158-62
Necessitarianism, 6-7, 68, 93-4
Necessity,
  logical and non-logical, 6-7, 56
  and certainty, Ch. 4, sect. 2 *passim*, 112
  and possibility, 6-7, Ch. 4, sect. 2 *passim*, 67-9, 77-8, 90-1, 93-4, 111-12, 171
  see also Laws of nature
Negligence, 22
Neurology, 131, 145, 161

Nomic possibility, see Possibility (2)
Nowell-Smith, P. H., 116-17, 123, 133, 135-7, 143, 154-5, 169

Obstacles, 147, 149, 153, 156, 162
Obstinacy, 115, 157
Occasion, 116, 121, 128
Ontological possibility, see Possibility (2)
Opportunity, 9, Ch. 6, sect. 2 *passim*, 116, 167
'Ought implies can', 126-7, 142-7, 151-5
Oxford English Dictionary, see Dictionary, Oxford English

Parallel cases, see Induction
Paranoia, 164
Particularity and universality, 23-4, 44-53, 76-7, 88-9, 92-3
Past experience, see Experience
Physiology, 161
Physique, 160
Popper, K., 29
Possibility, kinds of, 12-14 *et passim*
Possibility (1) (possibility for choice, personal power),
  and relative possibility, Ch. 2 *passim*, 106, 112, 171
  and natural possibility, 38, 75, Ch. 6 *passim*, 127-8, 158-62, 169-70
  orthodox analysis of, Ch. 7, sects. 3-5 *passim*
  knowledge of, see Trying
  and dispositions, Ch. 6, sect. 3 *passim*, 125, 127, 135, Ch. 7, sect. 4 *passim*, 143
  alleged conditionality of, Ch. 7, sect. 2 *passim*
  psychological, 148, 160-1
  physical, 160-3
  general capacity and opportunity, Ch. 6, sect. 2 *passim*
  and will, Ch. 7 *passim*, Ch. 8, sect. 2 *passim*

INDEX

Possibility (2) (natural possibility and power),
  and relative possibility, Ch. 3 *passim*
  and possibility for choice, *see* Possibility (1)
  analysis of, Ch. 4, sects. 4 and 5 *passim*, Ch. 5, sects. 1–3 *passim*, 103–4, 111–12, 125, 128, 140
  and necessity, *see* Necessity
  knowledge of, Ch. 4 *passim*
  particular and general, 52–3, 75–7, 92–3
  alleged conditionality of, Ch. 5, sect. 5 *passim*, 104–5, 119–22
  and actuality, *see* Actualism
Possibility (3) (relative or epistemic),
  and absolute possibility, *see* Possibility (1) *and* (2)
  explanation of, Chs. 2 and 3 *passim*
  difference from probability, 34, Ch. 3, sect. 4 *passim*
Possibility (4) (logical), 12, 27–8, 40, 50, 127, 171–2, 176, 178
'Possible', meaning of, *see* Ambiguity, Etymology *and* Senses, multiplication of
'Possible for' and 'possible that', 13–14, Ch. 2, sects. 4 and 5 *passim*, 38, 70, 158
Post-hypnotic suggestion, 164
Potentiality, *see* Possibility (2)
Powers, *see* Possibility (1) *and* (2)
  active and passive, 96, 105
Prediction,
  defence of, 22, 36
  of actions, Ch. 2, sect. 4 *passim*, 106, 115, 138, 140–1
  Hume on, 57–9
Preference, 137
Prevention 105, 158, 163; *see also* Obstacles, Difficulty and Excuses
Probability,
  and evidence, 17–26, 43–9
  'everyday' statements of, 19–25, 43–4, 46, 49
  and possibility, 16–18, 34, Ch. 3, sect. 4 *passim*, 59, 66
  alleged subjectivity of, 15–17, 23
  legal concept of, 22, 25
  and action, 23
  and expressions of intention, 33, 49
  of *a priori* propositions, 40, 49
Probability statements,
  identity of, 26
  hypothetical, 48–9
  particular and general, 25–6, 44–9, 51–2
'Probable', meaning of, 23, Ch. 3, sect. 3 *passim*, 54
Provocation, 165
Pseudo-conditionals, Ch. 5, sect. 5 *passim*, 104–5, Ch. 7, sect. 2 *passim*, 125, 128–9, 132, 148, 153, 174
Psychopaths, 168
Punishment, *see* Responsibility

Rationalism, 56–9
Realism, 60–3, 66–7, 74
Reasons,
  for belief, *see* Evidence *and* Prediction
  for acting, 30, 153–8, 162
Reductionism, 60, 66–7, 69
Relational properties, 84–5, 140
Responsibility, 2, 4, 10, 19, 120, 149, Ch. 8, sect. 3 *passim*
  utilitarian theory of, 126–7, 142–4, 148, 151–5
  shared, 165
  diminished, 164
  legal, 168–9
Ryle, Gilbert, 29, 35–6, 85, 106–18, 140–1

Scepticism, 3, 28–9, 34, 57, 60, 63–8, 73, 169–70
Schlick, M., 143
Self-control, 163–4

Senses, multiplication of, 46, 50–1, 85, 95, 113, 143, 172, 178; *see also* Ambiguity
Sensible Qualities, 57–8, 61–3, 86–7
Situation, change in,
 and probability, 21
 and possibility, 91–3
Skills, 108–11
Sleep, 115, 163, 168
Species and genus, 101, 110, 174, 176, 178
Spinoza, 57
Square of opposition, 176–7
Stevenson, C. L., 125–6, 131, 133, 135, 143, 169
Stimulus and reaction, 138, 141–3, 162
Stout, A. K., 30
Strata of potentiality, 85
Strawson, P. F., 78–9
Structure, 86–7
Stupidity, 168
Subjunctive, 70, 72–5, 123–4
Success, *see* Failure *and* Trying
Syllogism, 47–8

Tests, 62–4, 70, 73, 78–9, 83, 85–6, 89, 93, 107, 129–30, 132–4, 140–4, Ch. 7, sect. 6 *passim*
Theoretical questions, 47–9
Threats, 156–7, 164
Transcendentalism, *see* Realism
'True', 49
Trying, 116, 124, Ch. 7, sect. 3 *passim*, 135–6, 142, Ch. 7, sect. 6 *passim*, 153, 160–2, Ch. 8, sect. 3 *passim*

Uncertainty, 13, 15–16, 27–33, 106, 112, 171
Unconditional consequent, 78–9
Universe, 93–4, 101
Upbringing, 166–7
Urmson, J. O., 43, 45
Utilitarian theory of responsibility, *see* Responsibility

Volitions, 3, 131–2, 135

Wanting (wishing, will) and possibility, Ch. 7 *passim*, Ch. 8, sect. 2 *passim*
Wittgenstein, 27–8, 36–7, 47

Zeno, 90, 169

For Product Safety Concerns and Information please contact our EU
representative GPSR@taylorandfrancis.com
Taylor & Francis Verlag GmbH, Kaufingerstraße 24, 80331 München, Germany

www.ingramcontent.com/pod-product-compliance
Lightning Source LLC
Chambersburg PA
CBHW052120300426
44116CB00010B/1743